Through the experiences of five biblical men—men ʟɪᴋᴇ
Moses—Chase shows how these instincts can lead men to destruction, oɪ ᴠʏ
faith, to something better. Through their failures and success, we learn and
mature with them. But these are not just stories. Chase offers practices by
which we learn to discipline our own instincts. You will learn to live Paul's
advice to the young man Timothy, "Keep a close watch on yourself and on
the teaching." Know your instinct and know what you have in Christ. That
is the way forward for men. Chase will show you the way.

MARK BATTERSON, lead pastor of National Community Church; *New
York Times* bestselling author of *The Circle Maker*

There are lot of mixed messages in our society about masculinity—what it
is, what it should be, what it shouldn't be, and even whether it's really "a
thing." God designed men to be masculine in the best sense of the word.
That requires harnessing our natural impulses and letting Him direct those
traits toward the full, thriving manhood that He intends for all of us. This
book is a great starting point.

JIM DALY, President, Focus on the Family

In my twenty-four years as a pastor, two tragic words have come to summa-
rize the affliction of many men: lonely and bored. As Thoreau once quipped,
"The mass of men lead lives of quiet desperation." Once they've settled in
to the routines and presumed "have-to's" of life—family, career, and maybe
church—it is common for men to replace adventure and dreams with other
things that numb and distract: television, internet surfing, pornography,
sports, workaholism, voyeurism, excessive eating and drinking, an affair, and
the like. In *The 5 Masculine Instincts*, Chase does a great job not only describing this sad state of affairs for many men but also paving a path forward for
men who desire a better, more excellent way. Whether you are a man or there
is a man that you care about, I highly recommend this work to you.

SCOTT SAULS, senior pastor of Christ Presbyterian Church in Nashville,
TN; author of *Befriend* and *Irresistible Faith*

Chase takes the mask of masculinity right off the face of culture. This book exposes the lie that true masculinity is discovered in what we do, or what we possess. It redirects our hearts to the joyful truth that masculinity, at its core, is found in who we are becoming. It shows us how to become more like Christ. So seriously, buy this book, read it, soak in it, and spread the word. This book is a MUST READ for every man—and every woman who loves a man.

RASHAWN COPELAND, founder of I'm So Blessed Daily; author of *No Turning Back*

Chase is pursuing a much-needed goal—to help shape and inspire a new generation of godly men. With his ear to Scripture and a keen eye on culture, Chase brings the lives of the Bible's men into our own. As a result, we are able to learn from them and discover a better kind of manhood. *The 5 Masculine Instincts* is a book we need.

BRAD LOMENICK, leadership consultant, speaker, founder of BLINC, and author of *The Catalyst Leader* and *H3 Leadership*

Have you noticed how little we talk about character these days—particularly as men? We talk about toxic traits and roles and responsibilities, but men I know struggle most with living up to the expectations they have for themselves. They don't know how to get better. What men need is a new conversation about Christian character. Chase has done just that. Chase helps men grow in character by addressing the masculine instincts directing their lives through nuanced engagement with Scripture and deep gospel clarity. *The 5 Masculine Instincts* will help you become a man of true Christian character.

LT. GEN. (RET) WILLIAM G. BOYKIN, founding member of the elite US Army Delta Force; US Deputy Undersecretary of Defense for Intelligence; author of *Man to Man: Rediscovering Masculinity in a Challenging World*

If ever there was a language, fashioned uniquely to men . . . invented just for them, Chase Replogle speaks it. This book is clear-headed, bold, and crisp. After nearly forty years in the publishing business, I've been told that men don't read books. Take a few minutes in this one and you will agree with me that this book is a happy exception. Men need to read this. I predict they will. I'm so glad I did.

ROBERT WOLGEMUTH, bestselling author

It's funny how as we grow older and live more of life we often end up with a foggier sense of who we are and where our lives are supposed to go—well, more tragic than funny, really. It leads us into so many misguided decisions and down wrong paths. This book is not a guide or a self-help book, which is good because our selves were what caused this confusion in the first place. Nor is it a sermon or a mandate. Instead, it's a reflection on purpose and direction, and identity woven through with biblical truth. For any disillusioned, post-idealist adults facing broken dreams or a confusing vision of the future, this book is for you and will be a help.

BARNABAS PIPER, pastor, author of *Help My Unbelief* and *The Curious Christian*, and cohost of *The Happy Rant* podcast

A ton of books are written each year, but truly exceptional books can be counted on one hand. This is one such book, and it is no accident. Chase Replogle is a gifted, engaging author who is a master storyteller, thorough researcher, and excellent interpreter and applier of biblical truth. To be a truly exceptional book, however, it also has to address a real issue with real substance. Never has masculinity faced the challenges it faces today—from without and from within. Chase takes these challenges head-on: no beating around the bush and no shortage of solid, biblically based guidance required to get us back on track. Thank you, Chase, for producing a book that men—indeed, our entire culture—is desperate for!

WAVE NUNNALLY, professor Emeritus of Early Judaism and Christian Origins, Evangel University / Assemblies of God Theological Seminary

Talking about manhood today has become strangely controversial. That leaves a lot of men stuck. How are we supposed to be better as men if the whole conversation is always drama? *The 5 Masculine Instincts* is our way forward. I've known Chase for a long time and I know the years of work he's given to this topic. You'll recognize it when you read the book. I can't wait for all the men I know to read it. It's what we need.

DAN BOEVER, professional Trick-shot Golf Entertainer and RE/MAX World Long Drive Champion (Sr. Division)

The 5 Masculine Instincts is a fresh look at men today compared with men in the Bible. The author states there are no biblical heroes per se—with the exception of Jesus. For the most part, these men were ordinary, which makes them relatable. Chase's descriptions are interesting, colorful, insightful—and realistic.

GENE GETZ, professor, radio host, and author of *The Measure of a Man*

Being a man can be a challenge. We are easily discouraged and easily distracted. But we are not alone in this. The Word of the living God has given us men who are just like us. Chase highlights some of the crucial instincts so many of us experience as men, showing us where the men of the Bible got it right and where they also failed. Today's world continues to twist the purpose of masculinity and manhood. This book is going to point you back in the right direction. Whether you're a man wise in years or still striving to be, I encourage you to pick up *The 5 Masculine Instincts* and rediscover a better manhood in Christ.

KORY KEETH, PRCA Rodeo Announcer

So many men default to action, decisiveness, and willpower. But like chasing a ghost on the battlefield, success can feel elusive. Men are worn out, discouraged, or even on the verge of giving up in their search for the abundant life that Jesus offers. For those who dare, *The 5 Masculine Instincts* invites readers to travel on an exciting adventure, a journey with many twists, turns, surprises—and rewards. Chase Replogle provides life-changing insights through masterful examination of the Bible's men. Serious seekers will discover that the victory they've been seeking all along is just ahead as they learn to trust and receive. *The 5 Masculine Instincts* is a must-read for the military community!

CHAPLAIN (COL) SCOTT MCCHRYSTAL (US ARMY, RET.), Managing Editor of the *Warrior's Bible*, former Senior Military Chaplain at West Point, and former Chaplain Endorser for the Assemblies of God

I love discovering treasures from unexpected sources. And what could be a more unexpected source for learning about a balanced, biblical self-image than the Old Testament stories of men like ourselves? But that's exactly what Chase Replogle has accomplished. In *The 5 Masculine Instincts*, he uncovers principles we can all find value in, from a source we didn't expect.

KARL VATERS, author, founder of NewSmallChurch.com, and blogger for *Christianity Today*

I deeply appreciate Chase's desire to refresh orthodoxy for the modern reader. His commitment to the gospel is clear, his ability to nuance spiritual truths with story is well-crafted, and the outcome of watching men like him fill the shoes God places them in is timely.

HEATH ADAMSON, author, speaker, and advocate; Chief of Staff, Convoy of Hope

THE 5 MASCULINE INSTINCTS

A Guide to Becoming a Better Man

CHASE REPLOGLE

MOODY PUBLISHERS
CHICAGO

Some content in this book was previously published on the author's website (pastorwriter.com).

Unless otherwise indicated, Scripture quotations are from the *ESV® Bible (The Holy Bible, English Standard Version®)*, Copyright © 2001 by Crossway, a publishing ministry of Good News Publishers. Used by permission. All rights reserved.

Scripture quotations marked (NIV) are taken from the Holy Bible, New International Version®, NIV®. Copyright © 1973, 1978, 1984, 2011 by Biblica, Inc.™ Used by permission of Zondervan. All rights reserved worldwide. www.zondervan.com The "NIV" and "New International Version" are trademarks registered in the United States Patent and Trademark Office by Biblica, Inc.™

Edited by Andrew J. Spencer
Interior design: Ragont Design
Cover design: Erik M. Peterson
Man covering face courtesy of Ayo Ogunseinde, Unsplash.
Cover photo of man with gold chain copyright © 2020 by mimagephotography / Shutterstock (253202137).
Cover photo of man with hat copyright © 2020 by santypan / Shutterstock (483363439).
Cover photo of grey-haired man copyright © 2020 by LightField Studios / Shutterstock (754621336).
Cover photo of bearded man copyright © 2020 by Body Stock / Shutterstock (1913632150).
All rights reserved for all of the above photos.
Author photo: Jessica Yates

Library of Congress Cataloging-in-Publication Data

Names: Replogle, Chase, author.
Title: The 5 masculine instincts : a guide to becoming a better man / Chase
   Replogle.
Other titles: The five masculine instincts
Description: Chicago : Moody Publishers, [2021] | Includes bibliographical
   references. | Summary: "By examining the lives of five men of the Bible,
   The 5 Masculine Instincts shows that your own instincts are neither
   curse nor virtue. Through exploring sarcasm, adventure, ambition,
   reputation, and apathy, you'll come to understand yourself and how your
   instincts can be matured into something better"-- Provided by publisher.
Identifiers: LCCN 2021043746 (print) | LCCN 2021043747 (ebook) | ISBN
   9780802425546 | ISBN 9780802476463 (ebook)
Subjects: LCSH: Masculinity--Religious aspects--Christianity. | Men
   (Christian theology) | Masculinity--Bibiical teaching. | Men in the
   Bible. | Bible--Biography. | BISAC: RELIGION / Christian Living / Men's
   Interests | RELIGION / Leadership
Classification: LCC BV4528.2 .R47 2021 (print) | LCC BV4528.2 (ebook) |
   DDC 248.8/42--dc23
LC record available at https://lccn.loc.gov/2021043746
LC ebook record available at https://lccn.loc.gov/2021043747

Originally delivered by fleets of horse-drawn wagons, the affordable paperbacks from D. L. Moody's publishing house resourced the church and served everyday people. Now, after more than 125 years of publishing and ministry, Moody Publishers' mission remains the same—even if our delivery systems have changed a bit. For more information on other books (and resources) created from a biblical perspective, go to www.moodypublishers.com or write to:

Moody Publishers
820 N. LaSalle Boulevard
Chicago, IL 60610

1 3 5 7 9 10 8 6 4 2

Printed in the United States of America

For my son, Will.

The LORD bless you and keep you;
the LORD make his face to shine upon you
and be gracious to you;
the LORD lift up his countenance upon you
and give you peace.

— Dad

CONTENTS

FOREWORD

In 2017, I wrote a book titled *Play the Man* because I recognized a growing problem: we had forgotten how to make men. I opened the book with a story of a church father named Polycarp. He had been personally discipled by the apostle John and was the bishop of the church at Smyrna. Polycarp was tracked down by bounty hunters, arrested, and dragged before a bloodthirsty crowd that cheered his execution. The Roman Proconsul demanded that Polycarp renounce Christ and pledge his allegiance to Caesar instead. Polycarp refused. He explained to his captors, "Eighty and six years have I served Him, and He has done me no wrong! How then can I blaspheme my King who saved me?"

The crowd chanted for death by beasts, but Polycarp was sentenced to fire. When his body proved miraculously immune to the flames, he was pierced in the side by a spear and bled to death before the crowd. It's a gruesome story of steadfast faith in the face of persecution, and it raises a few questions for me. What is it that enables a man to die like that? Where does a man find the courage to overcome his own instinct for survival and give his life for something better? The answer is a voice from heaven that was heard by everyone in the stadium that day: "Be strong, Polycarp. Play the man."

Those divine words echo with the revelation of Scripture. As the dying King David passed his throne to his son, Solomon, he offered similar advice to him, "Be strong, and show yourself a man."

It has never been harder to live out David's advice or embrace Polycarp's masculine resolve. Right now, so much about being a man seems confusing. What is a man? How do we go about making them? How do we show ourselves to be one? Our culture recognizes what's wrong with men, but it rarely offers them a better way. I see it in the men I know and pastor. There is a restlessness about who God has called men to be. Men don't know how to get better.

Chase understands men and the challenges we face. He is a pastor and a reader, and it shows. Weaving together history, psychology, literature, and a rich narrative approach to Scripture, Chase offers you a guide for better understanding your own masculinity and learning to mature it into something better. This book will help you learn what those men of old once knew. It will teach you how to be a man, and not only a better man—a man of God.

The Five Masculine Instincts identifies five common masculine experiences. Reading the book, I immediately recognized these instincts in myself. These instincts are the raw material of masculinity. This is what we must learn to work with. Through the experiences of five biblical men—men like David, Samson, and Moses—Chase shows how these instincts can lead men to destruction or, by faith, to something better. Through their failures and successes, we learn and mature with them. But these are not just stories. Chase offers practices by which we learn to discipline our own instincts. You will learn to live Paul's advice to the young man Timothy, "Keep a close watch on yourself and on the teaching." Know your instinct and know what you have in Christ. That is the way forward for men. Chase will show you the way.

* * *

After Polycarp's death, many reflected on how he had died and how he had prayed in the face of suffering. Many repented and came to believe in Polycarp's Christ. His death strengthened a church facing persecution. I imagine many men were made that day. They were made as they witnessed Polycarp play the man so well. Stories of faith are powerful like that. Stories of men willing to live for better things inspire us to be better too.

I hope you read this book and learn from it, but I also hope you pass it along to your sons and grandsons, to your father, and your friends. We are all in this together. The more we understand our instincts, the more we can help one another grow into true Christlikeness, into a better manhood.

Mark Batterson
Lead pastor of National Community Church; *New York Times* best-selling author of *The Circle Maker*

Chapter 1

MEN, MEAT, AND THE MASCULINE MALAISE

"I call this turf 'n' turf. It's a 16 oz. T-bone and a 24 oz. porterhouse. Also, whisky and a cigar. I am going to consume all of this at the same time because I am a free American."

RON SWANSON

"Man has always lost his way. He has been a tramp ever since Eden; but he always knew, or thought he knew, what he was looking for. For the first time in history he begins really to doubt the object of his wanderings on the earth. He has always lost his way; but now he has lost his address."

G. K. CHESTERTON

This book is about masculinity, but honestly, I'm getting tired of talking about masculinity. Maybe it's because I became a man in a world where talking about masculinity was the least masculine thing a man could do. Or perhaps it's because the topic has become so hostile and combative it's hard to keep it from turning into another online shouting match. These days, masculinity seems to have very little to do with who a man actually is. It's about politics and culture, brands and evolution, liberals and conservatives, labels and stereotypes. There are only sides to take and a long list of ways to try and publicly prove it.

You've heard it all before. There are the obvious masculine tropes: beer, sports, women, guns, and cars. There are the old cautions of money, sex, and power. And there are the new cries of toxicity challenging masculine aggression, stoicism, and competition. But these conversations are all about symptoms—surface clichés. What they leave confused in the chaos of their wake are the everyday lives of the actual men I know. The real questions of masculinity lie much deeper than our culture's interest or opinions. And I'm afraid the questions are more complex than we may realize.

Let me give you an example of just how deep and just how complex the real conversations are. Let's talk about men and their instinct for meat.

* * *

I had never seen hives until rolling back my sleeves and discovering my arms covered in them. In twenty-four hours, they had spread to my back and chest. A few hours more, and they were on my face.

I've never been allergic to anything: not pollen, mold, peanuts, or shellfish, not even poison ivy, but my doctor was convinced I was having an anaphylactic reaction to something we couldn't identify. For three weeks, I had been growing steadily worse as we frantically changed shampoo, laundry detergent, toothpaste, deodorant, and vitamins, searching for something, anything. Still, each day the symptoms worsened. It had to be something I was eating.

Still miserable and covered in hives, I laid there trying to remember everything I had eaten over the last few days. Three days ago, my wife had made chili. Then I had ordered a burger from the Wendy's drive-through. Yesterday, it had been venison tacos—every year, I harvest and process a deer myself, loading our garage freezer with pounds of packaged deer meat and two back-straps—in my opinion, the best cut of meat in the world. There is nothing like a perfectly cooked medium-rare deer tenderloin, but I digress.

That's when I had a terrible thought. Can you develop an allergy to meat? Surely not. We had already tried cutting out dairy and gluten and a whole list of strange but apparently common food allergens. "God help me if I'm allergic to a bacon cheeseburger," I thought.

As I had done so many times over the last three weeks, I reached for my phone and began googling.

* * *

In 2014, the University of Hawaii at Manoa published results of an experiment on men's relationship with meat and masculinity.[1] One hundred and fifty men were selected to test an online pizza-ordering app. At least that's what they were told. Each man would be given a list of ingredients and asked to build their personalized pizza. They had no idea that they were really participating in a complex inquiry into their identity, which would seek to manipulate and expose the vulnerabilities of their masculinity.

Before placing their pizza order, each conducted a personality assessment that included questions about their conforming to certain gender traits. Regardless of their answers, they were given one of two predetermined results. Half were informed they had scored higher than most men. The other half were told they scored lower than most men and had answered more in line with female participants. Their answers didn't actually matter. The researchers manipulated the results, so half of the participants would experience what they called a "masculinity threat condition."[2]

Having their manhood "scientifically" questioned, they were next tasked with ordering their pizza. The list of ingredients had been carefully tested on a control group and was categorized by two types: meats and vegetables. They included things like steak, bacon, and pepperoni as well as eggplant, olives, broccoli, and artichoke hearts.

What did the researchers discover? The men who had their masculinity questioned were statistically more likely to pile on meat. Or, as the study concluded, "Following the male identity threat manipulation, men were in general more likely to increase their intended meat intake."[3] Eating more meat helped men feel better about having their masculinity questioned. Having eaten meat, they felt more like men again.

Believe it or not, there is a growing body of academic research that associates the consumption of meat with masculinity. And it's not just being proved through university experiments. According to the US Department of Health and Human Services, American men eat 57 percent more meat than women, significantly more than the US Dietary Guidelines recommend.[4]

Why are men ordering more burgers and steaks? That's actually a very complicated question to answer. Some researchers believe that the association is strictly cultural and created through a pervasive consumer-driven caricature of men. You might remember that 2007 Burger King ad that depicted men marching in the street chanting, "I am man and I'm way too hungry to settle for chick food." Burger King was advertising its new Texas Double Whopper. Those commercials concluded, "Eat like a man, man."

Other researchers find a much older explanation for men's meat infatuation. Some biologists locate the association of men and meat with the development of the masculine emphasis on hunting. They describe changes in the bones of males and females from the Neolithic period, which seem to show females eating more wheat and barley while men began an increased consumption of red meat. Some have even identified this milestone as the birth of patriarchy.[5]

It gets more problematic. Our culture is also split on whether eating meat is the antidote to various forms of degenerative health issues or if eating meat is actually the disease that is destroying our planet and risking the future of humanity itself. I'm not being hyperbolic. Take, for example, the recent wave of men adopting the controversial Carnivore diet. Adherents are permitted to eat only meat, salt, and water. Proponents have described a long list of benefits, including increased and sustained energy and a general decrease in depression.

But others see their miracle diet as a curse. The British Independent news agency recently published an article entitled, "Fragile masculinity says meat is manly. If we don't challenge that, people will die and the earth will be irreversibly damaged."[6] The author argues that a toxic form of masculinity is keeping us from adopting the necessary vegan diet required to solve global warming. I told you this would get complicated.

One thing should be clear enough: we can't even agree on what men should eat. Men, by their instinct for more meat, are either responding to evolutionary law, chasing a cultural fad, brainwashed by corporate marketers, or passively risking all of human existence. If the contents of the brown bag you take for lunch cause this much debate, anxiety, and uncertainty, what else is controversial and confusing about being a man today? The answer: a lot.

* * *

Oh, and it turns out you can become allergic to meat. As my hive-induced google searching soon uncovered, there is a tick-born disease called alpha-gal—also known as The Mammalian Meat Allergy. Yes, a tick bite can leave you allergic to all things mammal. According to the Wikipedia page, it was rare but was documented in my geographic area.

That's when I remembered. A few weeks before my symptoms began, I had removed two ticks from my ankle, and the next day discovered a third still on the back of my leg. My doctor recommended I immediately stop eating all mammal meat and dairy products. A couple of days later, my symptoms were gone. I had alpha-gal. I was allergic to meat.

I quickly discovered that meat is in just about everything. Marshmallows and medication, toothpaste and deodorants, most chewing gum and anything cross-contaminated by the minimum-waged 16-year-old in the kitchen who just cut your veggie sandwich with the same knife he used to cut your friend's ham sandwich. I have since been introduced to all the "vegan" alternatives: tofu, tempeh, seitan, everything soy and almond, and a strange packet of grayish strips called vegan "bacon."

When I explain my situation, most men have the same reaction, "I'd rather die." They are joking—I think. My dad once suggested I drive to Amarillo and try that 72-ounce steak challenge.

"It will either kill you or purge it out of your system," he said. He was joking—I think.

THE MASCULINE MALAISE

The list of masculine instincts men experience is much longer than their craving for meat but there seems to be just two ways men are being instructed to respond to those instincts. There are those who see traditionally masculine instincts as toxic and those who see them as salvific.

Based on what are perceived to be destructive masculine stereotypes and attributes—now called toxic masculinity—many in our culture continue to call for a deconstructing of masculinity, replacing it with an alternative list of less "dangerous" attributes. The American Psychological Association explained in a controversial 2019 publication, "Traditional masculinity—marked by stoicism, competitiveness, dominance and aggression—is, on the whole, harmful. Men socialized in this way are less likely to engage in healthy behaviors."[7]

> Men are constantly left on the defensive, often not sure what they are defending, but feeling threatened nonetheless.

However, the energy with which society has embraced the toxic masculinity mantra has been met by an equally energized counterreaction. There are many who think traditionally masculine instincts shouldn't be abandoned but pursued and indulged. They suspect the charge of toxicity is really an attack on manhood itself. They point to celebrities and politicians declaring that the "future is female" to prove their skepticism of anyone wanting to "cure" man's toxic traits.

As the debate has intensified, masculinity has slipped into depersonalized parodies. We end up with cartoon characterizations of men, flimsy carboard cutout heroes and propped-up strawman opponents. We compress the full experience of manhood into catchphrases and protest slogans. We speak of masculinity as if it were a brand men could like on Facebook or a sticker across the back of their pickups and Priuses. Men are constantly left on the defensive, often not sure what they are defending, but feeling threatened nonetheless. There is no way forward, only trenches to dig deeper.

Michael Ian Black lamented the way in which this lack of clarity is robbing men of what it means to be a man. He writes, "To be a girl today is to be the beneficiary of decades of conversation about the complexities of womanhood, its many forms, and expressions. Boys, though, have been left behind. No commensurate movement has emerged to help them navigate toward a full expression of their gender. It's no longer enough to 'be a man'—we no longer even know what that means."[8]

You probably remember the 2019 Gillette Super Bowl commercial, which repositioned the company's slogan from "the best a man can get" to "the best a man can be." The commercial sparked immediate controversy with its references to the #MeToo movement, bullying, and sexism.

The commercial pictured men making unwanted passes at women, belittling their female colleagues at work, and condoning childhood bullying as a means to toughness. Depicted as an endless line of men behind their grills, they echoed the refrain, "boys will be boys." The final line of the ad read, "It's only by challenging ourselves to do more that we can get closer to our best." The commercial did what most of our conversations about masculinity do; it called men to try harder, to do more, and to make themselves better. But the question so rarely asked is how? How do we do better? Is it really as simple as trying harder? Are men monsters simply for a lack of effort? Can men be cured by marketing campaigns?

Our culture has become highly skilled in pointing out the problems, but, beyond public service campaigns and news headlines, we haven't developed the same expertise in helping men solve those problems. We have lost the wisdom by which men become better, by which they mature into a better manhood.

We have come to believe that men can simply be changed from the outside. That with enough social pressure or shame or advertising dollars we can convince them to behave. Both sides see men's problems as external. Both see the challenges as cultural conflicts. Both see the other as man's greatest threat. They each have their ideal but only accusation and protest to obtain them. Neither offers a path for producing what they believe in. They rely on slogans, celebrities, and the power of social pressure—great for gathering crowds, stirring up online debates, and garnering votes, but not very helpful for cultivating individual character.

Unfortunately, the church has not done much better. Desperate to attract men and keep their attention, we've turned conversations about manhood into similarly extreme litmus tests of masculine interests: beards, bacon, and blowing things up. When more serious, we too have focused almost exclusively on the external behavior of men, defining masculinity by what men should and shouldn't do. We call men to become better husbands, fathers, and church volunteers. It's not that those expectations are wrong, but expectations themselves don't make men better.

Marriage is no cure for a lustful heart, and having a child doesn't guarantee your own maturity. You can't confer character by a title or job description. And simply giving men more responsibility doesn't guarantee they'll suddenly form the virtues necessary to bear it.

Similarly, our conversations about Christian manhood usually turn into more debate: positions on submission, leadership, and authority. Men take sides and think the accuracy of their theological position is enough to secure their manhood. Those conversations do matter, but when they come before conversations on character, they tend to stunt growth rather than inspire it. Most of the men I know do want to be great husbands, fathers, and friends. They want to bear greater responsibility and serve others well too, but it's their own sense of inadequacy at the task that tends to hold them back.

In many ways, the Gillette commercial was right. Far too many men are wrong, far too many do practice and condone indefensible behavior, but the commercial and so many of our own conversations fall short of offering a better way. Men are confused about how to get better. And they are confused about what better even means. The constant barrage of accusation and outrage does not produce the character it seeks but rather defensiveness, resentment, and indifference, all poison to the real work of character. It's so much easier to give up and fall back to whatever feels right—to fall back to your instincts.

I've long been haunted by a line in one of Walker Percy's novels. "Men are dead, dead, dead; and the malaise has settled like a fall-out and what people really fear is not that the bomb will fall but that the bomb will not fall . . . I know nothing and there is nothing to do but fall prey to desire."[9] We become nothing more than what we feel. We become our instincts.

Some can articulate it; they can talk about this experience of moral discouragement and disillusionment. Others express it only through their disengagement, too often coping through substance abuse, escaping through fantasy, pornography, and video games, or vicariously living out the success of sports teams and politicians.

So many are caught in this malaise. An uneasiness, a weariness, an unshakable sense that so much is wrong, that nothing really matters, and nothing can really be done about it anyway. Longing for something meaningful while simultaneously laughing at those who believe in such things. We give up on getting better, settling into this malaise as just the way we are as men. Indulging our raw instincts and questioning anyone who would question us, everything seemingly hostile. We're not sure what else to do with what we feel, afraid to admit we feel at all. We defend what we never really chose. We pick fights to avoid ourselves. Make enemies to have something worth fighting for. All of it an indulgence in this instinctive unease. What else is there to guide us?

In what is perhaps the most dangerous mistake of all, we come to think that mindless indulgence in our instincts is the proof of our masculinity, that what we feel must be our deepest truth; to risk any kind of introspection, a threat to manhood itself. We come to think that this male malaise is masculinity. To indulge is masculine. To question your instincts is only to take the bait and jeopardize the whole game.

WHAT TO DO WITH YOUR INSTINCTS

It has never been more important to develop the skills necessary to recognize your instincts. C. S. Lewis wrote that human instincts are "an unreflective or spontaneous impulse."[10] Instincts don't require forethought or decision. They don't require us to even know they are there to affect us. We have not chosen them or reasoned our way to their existence, yet they speak to us with a weight of conviction. An instinct is a way of perceiving who you are, the world you are in, and how you should act in the midst of it.

> Every soldier knows there is a time to fight and a time to retreat. The real question is which is true at this moment.

Our feeling these instincts, sometimes profoundly, seems to be enough evidence for trusting them. These instincts influence everything we do in small and profound ways. No one has time to draw up a cost/benefit analysis for every decision, so we trust our instincts to guide us. Lewis described them as "Behaviour as if from knowledge."[11] We act as if we knew what we were doing. But if you have never thought about what instincts might be guiding you, you don't know what you're doing. You act as if from knowledge.

The question, too often unanswered, is whether any particular instinct should be checked or trusted.[12] Instincts can be wrong. Every soldier knows there is a time to fight and a time to retreat. The real question is which is true at this moment. Trust only your instinct and you are prone to making the wrong choice. You need more than what you feel to live well. A soldier is made by discipline, not impulse.

I'm convinced this is the challenge costing too many men a better manhood. In a world of individualized truth and hyper-defensiveness, we've lost the ability to decide what to do with our instincts. We have failed to become their master. Instead, they rule us.

The philosopher Fredrich Nietzsche suggested, "An instinct is weakened when it rationalises itself."[13] When you force your instincts to explain themselves, they suddenly lose some of their power to control you. It's time to put your instincts to a test. It's time to ask them some tough questions.

So, what are these instincts, robbing so many men of a better manhood? I want to offer you five of these masculine instincts and five biblical men who have struggled with them, men who by their successes and failures can show us a better way. They are our guides to a better manhood.

Chapter 2

LEARNING TO RECOGNIZE YOUR INSTINCTS

"Ideas pull the trigger, but instinct loads the gun."

DON MARQUIS

"Purity does not mean crushing the instincts but having the instincts as servants and not the master of the spirit."

ERIC LIDDELL, *The Disciplines of the Christian Life*

Shakespeare is remembered as one of the world's great commentators on human nature. His work captured more than dramatic situations; it captured the drama and complexity of the human heart. His play *As You Like It* contains one of Shakespeare's most famous lines. "All the world's a stage, and all the men and women merely players." Shakespeare continued, "One man in his time plays many parts."[1]

The play goes on to outline what is known as the Seven Stages of a Man. Shakespeare wanted to capture the passions and instincts that shape men. He counted seven of these unique instinctive stages.

Stages one and seven—the two bookends—are intentionally alike. A man begins as an infant, whimpering and puking in his nurse's arms. Similarly, men, in their final days, become once again dependent on a nurse's care. They often lose their speech, teeth, vision, and continence like before in infancy. Shakespeare called it the "second childishness." He meant to highlight that as we come, so we go.

What fascinates me are the five middle stages—those that depict the child maturing into full adulthood—and the five instincts that motivate him: sarcasm, adventure, ambition, reputation, and apathy.

SARCASM

The first stage is the boy, dressed for school but dragging his feet, whining and reluctant to take on the responsibility of learning the ways of the world. He is not just young by age, but by his immaturity and his unwillingness to grow up. His jokes and antics are a cover for contempt. He is quick to complain, convinced the world is unfair, and desperate to avoid the burden of knowing. Instead, he lives by what he feels. His sarcasm is an instinct which leaves him vulnerable to his own ignorance.

ADVENTURE

In the second of the stages, Shakespeare described man as a lover. He is driven by passion and idealism. His is the world of romance and quests. His instinct is to go, to travel off to the horizon in search of his true identity, heroic exploit, and love. Shakespeare likened him to a sighing furnace, burning within and thwarted without. His instinct is for the pursuit of adventure.

AMBITION

The third stage is the soldier's. His instinct is for oaths and honor. His vision of sacred purpose carries him onto battlefields and into the world's pressing conflicts. He believes he is capable of righting wrong. He is quick to quarrel and quick to make demands, always with an opinion and passionate belief. Believing he is destined for something great, he is prone to visions which cast his sight constantly into the future. His instinct is the pursuit of his ambition.

REPUTATION

By stage four, the man has found enough success and money to become interested in his reputation and comfort. Shakespeare even recognized that by this stage, he had usually begun to put on some extra weight—I'm not pointing any fingers. He learns to dress and properly cut his beard, now conforming to the expectations of society. He becomes who he is expected to be and determined to protect his hard-earned respectability. His instinct is to guard his reputation.

APATHY

By stage five, he has grown tired of all this work and complexity. The "world is too wide," as Shakespeare put it. With age, his voice has begun to fade; it is symbolic of his engagement with the world. His vision is dulled. He is most comfortable in his slippers and recliner. He doesn't venture out as much as he used to. Content with his hobbies and luxuries, he knocks around the house. The world is complex, and by his experience, the recognition of inadequacy and mortality cannot be ignored. His instinct is to protect his autonomy and to disengage from what he cannot control. His highest purpose is to be left alone. His instinct is for apathy.

* * *

Shakespeare imagined these instincts as ages. Men progressed through them as they grew in years. But these ages don't need to correspond to a man's biological age. These ages are the times a man finds himself in. They are not always chronological and often more than one is present. What Shakespeare captured were the underlying instincts that so many men experience without ever considering. Obviously, life and instincts are more complicated than this limited list, but my guess is, you found yourself resonating with parts of Shakespeare's descriptions.

It didn't take me long to start recognizing them, not only in the men I know, but also in the men of the Bible I've spent so much of my life studying. There are numerous examples for each, but I've chosen to focus on these five:

- Cain, the reluctant school-boy
- Samson, the wandering adventurer
- Moses, frustrated by ambition
- David, desperate to protect his reputation
- Abraham, tested by his own disengagement and apathy

I want to show you that the men of the Bible offer us an experience of masculine instincts capable of helping us recognize and challenge our own. Or, as Paul Taylor explained it, "We learn from fiction in something like the way we learn directly from life."[2] Their experiences can serve as our own. We can learn their lessons without the pain of having to learn them on our own. If true of fiction, how much more from these biblical stories of actual men?

If you're having a hard time understanding why your life is a mess, why you constantly fall prey to the same sins, or why you can't seem to make meaningful progress, perhaps you've failed to recognize the instincts you've been following. You are not alone. The Bible is full of men just like you, confused and struggling to figure out their own instincts.

Their stories are a powerful tool for understanding your own life. Eugene Peterson explained: "We enter these stories and recognize ourselves as participants, whether willing or unwilling, in the life of God."[3] There is a reason I'm turning to these biblical stories to discuss your instincts. There is a reason I've chosen stories over a list of rules or clever steps to take. A story is the best way to slip past the defenses of your instincts and discover a better way.

But before you can recognize their instincts and fully appreciate their stories, we need to address the way we've been reading about masculinity in the Bible. Go looking for the wrong thing and you risk finding it.

THEY ARE HUMANS, NOT HEROES

Ancient societies were prolific in producing heroes for their men to follow. Those ancient heroes articulated who society needed men to be. Proper masculine role models created men, so the ancient world offered a pantheon of masculine ideals. They did not tell the story of actual men but of aspirations. They told heroic tales of men like Odysseus, Hercules, and Achilles.

It's easy to imagine ancient Greek boys growing up with images of these men in their minds. Look like them. Act like them. Become a man like them. Possibly even die like them, but by so doing acquire their honor and glory. This is what any Greek boy could aspire to become. Heroic stories became the foundation of Greek and Roman culture, their identity as a people, their aspirations as adolescents.

We naturally think that the Bible offers similar but distinctly Christian alternatives to those heroic lives to inspire us and show us our own path toward proper manhood. After all, the Bible is full of men. We slap these biblical figures on flannel boards, imagining them as our own pantheon of greats. We hope they can serve as our own masculine role models. They had Hercules; we have Samson. They had Hector; we have David. They had Odysseus; we have Abraham. But as we spend time in these biblical stories, we soon find that the Bible isn't very good at meeting our expectations for heroes. Sure, you can imagine men like Moses as a hero, standing toe to toe against the most powerful ruler in the world. David fearless before giants. Or Abraham, who set out on the adventure of a lifetime and fathered a nation.

The biblical stories are not there to inspire us but to expose us.

But those are only selective memories of their lives. Their full stories are filled with fear, insecurity, anger, misdirection, disappointments, and devastating sins. Moses was constantly afraid and frustrated. David was prone to malicious cover-ups. Abraham lost his patience and splintered the family tree into generations of hostility. Would we even welcome these men to our stages?

Would we call their lives heroic if they lived today? The Bible, as it turns out, tells the story of humans, not heroes. Complicated and compromised humans. That's good news for us as men.

Literary scholar Erich Auerbach points out just how unique the ancient Israelites were in their approach to storytelling. "The Scripture stories do not, like Homer's, court our favor, they do not flatter us that they may please us and enchant us—they seek to subject us. . . . Far from seeking, like Homer, merely to make us forget our own reality for a few hours, it seeks to overcome our reality: we are to fit our own life into its world."[4] The biblical stories are not there to inspire us but to expose us.

The Israelite storytellers weren't interested in creating stock role models or masculine ideals; they were interested in waking Israel to what was going on around them and in them. These biblical lives are far more like us than most of us want to admit.

It is the complexity of the biblical lives and instincts that invite each of us into a deeper reading of their stories and our own. That is their power and their gift to us. There are no easy applications or moral platitudes, but if you keep their stories alive—in all their complexity—you will find them to be remarkable companions and fellow travelers on this path toward God.

I'm fond of the word "companion." It reminds me of the men walking together on the road to Emmaus: walking, discussing, and trying to figure out the meaning of Jesus' life and death. They were together in their doubts, in their discoveries, and in their culminating recognition of Christ resurrected. The men of the Bible are with us on that journey too—beside us, not ahead of us. As Jesus put it, they were longing to see his day, straining by faith to be in on it (Matt. 13:17). We are in it with them. Our aim is not to be like Moses or to become more like David.

THE 5 MASCULINE INSTINCTS

They are not the end at which we aim our lives. They point us to something better. They point us to Christ.

Our goal is not just to be men, but to be men becoming more like Christ. He is our aim. If there is a hero in this story, it is Him alone. There is no biblical manhood that does not ultimately lift our eyes toward Him. That pursuit unites us and binds us with those men and women of Scripture. We are all aiming at Christlikeness.

THE CHARACTERISTICS OF MASCULINITY

If Christ is the aim of all, both men and women, should conversations about gender matter? Is it worth the time and controversy to take up the subject? I think so. I think it matters far more than we've realized, because knowing the destination is only a part of the work required to get you there.

I love to sail. My wife and I have a small sailboat on a lake not far from our house. I also love to read about sailing, particularly books about long ocean passages. There is a common course many sailors will take from the west coast of California to Hawaii, usually a two-to-three-week trip. Getting to Hawaii by sail requires some unexpected decisions. Often, sailors are forced to sail away from Hawaii to get there. It's not uncommon for them to begin by sailing almost due south, trying to pick up the Pacific trade winds to carry them more quickly to the west.

If you are on a 200,000-ton cruise ship, you can point the bow at Honolulu and be there in less than a week, but a sailboat's characteristics require completely different tactics for reaching that same port. Both ships may have the same destination, but the courses necessary to get there have everything to do with the characteristics of the vessel they man and the captain's working knowledge of his own ship.

I think that's a good way of thinking about the task before us as men and women following Christ and growing in His character. Our destination is not some masculine cliché or some cultural stereotype of what a man should be. We seek to be like Christ, whom we follow. But to follow Him well requires the maturity to understand the characteristics of ourselves—our biology, experiences, impulses, and instincts—and, like a skilled ship captain, how to work those characteristics toward that goal. It's knowing what to do with your masculine instincts that makes you a better man.

C. S. Lewis similarly described two ways this "human machine" can go wrong. He used an analogy, suggesting you imagine a fleet of ships setting out to traverse an ocean and arrive together at a distant port.[5] The first and arguably most critical decision is to identify the intended destination. Lewis called this the morality of purpose. But Lewis recognized two more fundamental questions remained, both critical for reaching that port.

First, the ships must carefully communicate to determine which position they will each take in relationship to the others. They stand little chance of arriving at their destination if they are constantly crashing into one another, each making navigational choices with no regard for the others. Lewis described this risk as "when human individuals drift apart from one another, or else collide with one another and do one another damage."[6] These are the external responsibilities of each man, and this is where most of our conversations with men have focused.

How should men behave in the workplace and at home? What are their responsibilities to family and community? What role should they play in church and among neighbors? But even if we could all agree on the answers to those questions and even if all men felt motivated to try, there is still another requirement to make our destination.

The ships must be in good enough working order to carry out the maneuvers and maintain the courses required of them. The captain of the ship may have all the necessary courses drawn up, but if he helms a ship with a shoddy rudder or an out-of-balance load, no compass or charted course can help him reach his destination. Sadly, many men have found themselves incapable of living up to even their own intentions.

As Lewis wisely recognized, these two questions depend on each other more than we often acknowledge. "You cannot have either of these two things without the other. If the ships keep on having collisions they will not remain seaworthy very long. On the other hand, if their steering gears are out of order they will not be able to avoid collisions."[7]

We need men to behave better among others, but we stand little chance of pulling off those maneuvers if men cannot maintain and guide the inner workings of their own vessels. We have asked men to set sail on ships they know very little about. We have offered them no course or education on stewarding those ships well. We have given them a goal, asked of them proper behavior, but failed to teach them what previous generations of men had access to—the means of cultivating personal character. Lewis called this the task of "tidying up or harmonising the things inside each individual."[8]

This missing skill has its aim not on ideals but on practical wisdom. Naming the parts of a man's soul—halyards and sheets, downhauls and outhauls—learning to trim the sails, scrubbing the decks, scraping off barnacles, recognizing dangerous weather patterns, and learning when to reef and when you must lie ahull. Each vessel has its quirks and personalities. The best sailor is not the man with the best ship; it's the man who understands his ship best and the tactics necessary to get that ship safely to its proper destination.

Each of us is a mixed bag of traits, instincts, genetics, and common experiences shared by many men but unique to each. Some men experience these instincts in traditionally masculine ways, while others find their experience of masculinity to fit the mold less precisely. But it's not the possession of these traits that makes you a man. It's the wisdom that can master whatever raw material you find yourself with and guide it toward Christlikeness.

There is no perfect ship, not for long anyway. Even the most luxurious yachts require constant cleaning and maintenance. What matters most is not the ship you've inherited but learning to man it well.

CHARACTER THROUGH SELF-AWARENESS AND GOSPEL-AWARENESS

The apostle Paul gave this advice to the young man Timothy: "Watch your life and doctrine closely. Persevere in them, because if you do, you will save both yourself and your hearers" (1 Tim. 4:16 NIV). His advice was for Timothy to pay particular attention to himself and the gospel. Paul wanted Timothy to receive all that Christ had offered, and understood that self-knowledge was a critical part of receiving it.

Paul spoke of this work as necessary for Timothy to progress and necessary to set an example for other believers. Christian character always requires these two types of attention: self-awareness and gospel-awareness. It is formed by what we have received from Christ and through our working out that good news in the context of our own identity, instincts, and experiences. We practice and progress in character as we become more self-aware and gospel-aware. That work always requires testing and endurance, but it will produce character. And it is character, according to Paul, that leads to hope, the assurance of reaching that distant port.

N. T. Wright has warned of the church's declining interest in character and the work required to cultivate it. He explains his concerns by pointing out the advice typically given to new believers. "Now that he has come to faith, people in his church expect him to behave in a particular way (and *not* to behave in other particular ways), but this is seen, not in terms of character, but in terms of straightforward obligation. In other words, Christians are *expected* to live by the rules. When they fail, as they will, they are simply to repent and try to do better next time. You either live a Christian life or you don't."[9]

We have been well warned of the consequences of sin, and rightfully so, but the best set of rules and self-willed discipline to avoid breaking them doesn't guarantee maturity or true character. We have learned what we are against but haven't developed the self-knowledge to mature into those better things worth living and sacrificing for. When we fail to teach men how to grow in character, we shouldn't be surprised to discover they lack it.

When Paul urged Timothy to watch his life and the teaching closely, he was offering Timothy a way of balancing his life through self-knowledge and knowledge of the gospel. Either pursued without the counterbalancing force of the other produces a thin veneer of a person prone to collapse. Obsess over self-knowledge and you will get lost in an endless maze of your own insecurities. But, perhaps surprisingly, there is an equal risk in ignoring self-knowledge and turning your spiritual life into the acquisition of biblical knowledge alone. A head full of properly defined theological affirmations will not guarantee character either. It's never just one thing.

C. S. Lewis cautioned against elevating "any one instinct or any set of instincts." Instead, he described moral character as "something which makes a kind of tune (the tune we call goodness or right conduct) by directing the instincts."

"The most dangerous thing you can do," wrote Lewis, "is to take any one impulse of your own nature and set it up as the thing you ought to follow at all costs. There is not one of them which will not make us into devils if we set it up as an absolute guide. You might think love of humanity in general was safe, but it is not. If you leave out justice you will find yourself breaking agreements and faking evidence in trials 'for the sake of humanity,' and become in the end a cruel and treacherous man."[10]

Character is the balancing of these instincts toward something better. The instincts I've described in this book are not necessarily sinful but if left unchecked and overindulged, they have the tendency to collapse a man's life into desperation and defeat. A desire for adventure is not sinful but if habitual and unchecked, it is prone to weakening your commitments and betraying you. Similarly, there is nothing sinful about ambition. Ambition has helped many men achieve good things, but when blindly indulged it tends toward anger, self-righteousness, and overwork. It will enslave you. All instincts are like that. The real risk is letting them go unchecked, driving you in their singular pursuit away from God's grace and to your own destruction. They may not be sinful but the turmoil they unleash leads many men to places they never imagined going.

What the men of the Bible offer us are depictions of these instincts—second-hand experiences of their actual failures, pains, and destruction—and a witness to the God who led them and guided them on to something better than their own impulses. By their example, we learn to better understand ourselves and the grace we too have received. We learn where to look for both, keeping a careful watch on our own lives and drinking deep of the power of the gospel for new life in Him.

The goal of this book is not to annihilate your masculine instincts or to pull them back to some safer middle ground. The goal is to help you recognize the proper counterbalances necessary to keep those instincts from leading you into collapse. What you need is enough self-knowledge to recognize your instinct and a counterweight—an intentional practice of faith—by which to balance it and experience the power of His grace. You need the work of developing character to help you steward the ship and see it safely to its final port. The men of the Bible are your companions for doing just that.

Chapter 3

SARCASM: THE HUMOR OF OUR AGE

THE CAIN STORY: GENESIS 4

"But when the question is, 'How shall man be just with God?' reason must be silent, revelation must speak; and he who will not hear it assimilates himself to the first deist, Cain; he may not kill a brother, he certainly destroys himself."

HENRY MELVILLE

"He never complained. He seemed to have no instinct for the making much of oneself that complaining requires."

WENDELL BERRY, *Jayber Crow*

Where is Abel your brother?" God asked (Gen. 4:9). Cain knew the answer. He had murdered him, lured him away from their home and rose up against him in the field, spilled his blood into the fresh soil of creation. Death had claimed its first victim not by age or disease but at the hand of a brother's resentment. A snapped neck or perhaps a rock to the skull. Cain knew. He knew exactly where his brother was, where his body now lay lifeless and cold.

Cain answered, "I do not know; am I my brother's keeper?" (Gen. 4:9). How shifty was Cain's response? His returned question was an answer without offering one. He must have thought he was pretty clever. Dark and derisive, he scoffed at responsibility itself. His sarcasm gave away his juvenile contempt, not just for his brother Abel but for God. Our English word "sarcasm" tracks back to an old Greek word for tearing at flesh. Cain had spilled his brother's blood, and by his sarcasm, he clawed at the authority of God's question too.

Some have called sarcasm the humor of our age. It may not be a sin, but sarcasm is often a cover for something far more complex. It is not always rolled eyes or clever jokes. It is often a tactic of avoidance, a way of speaking without having to speak, of acting without the risk of action. Offering a part in order to hold back the whole. It is a form of concealment. John Haiman, a linguist and author of *Talk Is Cheap: Sarcasm, Alienation, and the Evolution of Language*, explains that people who use sarcasm are not usually kidding. The joke is often a means of protection. Sarcasm is a survival technique for the insecure.[1] Or as Gene Forrester describes himself in *A Separate Peace*, "I recognized sarcasm as the protest of people who are weak."[2] He wasn't describing physical weakness, but sarcasm as a protest against what we feel incapable of controlling. Sarcasm is usually contempt.

Some have proposed that sarcasm begins as a developmental milestone in which a child's rudimentary lies take on a more refined approach to testing the boundaries of truth. It is a sign of adolescence, an embryonic maturity which has learned to conceal falsehood with clever speech. Adam and Eve hid from God when they first felt guilt—a childish response and characteristic of their inexperience with sin. Cain's sarcasm served the same deceitful purpose (concealing the truth) but he imagined himself more shrewd, more evolved. He hid not behind a bush but behind his own wit. His first instinct was a form of sarcasm which protected himself and rejected the lesson God was offering.

Shakespeare described this instinctive reluctance as the schoolboy's complaint, an aversion to learning and an immature disdain. Sarcasm is usually a sign of immaturity and, when threatened, it is an instinct to avoid responsibility. Thus, Cain, in his immaturity, refused the divine lesson at hand. Sarcasm imagines every lesson to be a threat. But how would Cain grow into the man God created him to be if every opportunity for growth was met by sarcastic jest?

Could your sarcasm, as funny as it may seem, be holding you back from a divine lesson, an opportunity to grow into something better? How does the reluctant schoolboy ever learn to be a man without giving up his complaint? When he is only looking for fun, how can he ever grow into something more? He must learn to recognize the divine threat for what it is: a divine rite of passage into mature manhood.

MATURITY AND GROWTH PAINS

Each year, in the early spring on a remote island in the Vanuatu Archipelago, a group of young men participate in a rite of passage known as land diving. Villagers gather to construct a makeshift wooden tower, often more than 100 feet tall. The young men take turns climbing the tower, tying a single vine to each of their feet, and then diving headfirst from its peak. In this ancient form of bungee jumping, men prove their courage by attempting to fall as close to the ground as possible before being abruptly caught by their jungle tethers.

Snapped vines often leave men with fractured bones and, on occasion, some even die. But each year, more men volunteer for the honor of hurling themselves toward the ground from those towers. It's easy to shake your head at such desperate attempts to prove manhood, but the truth is, I've done some pretty stupid things to try and prove mine and usually to impress girls who never seemed all that impressed.

A few weeks before getting married, while serving as counselors at our church's youth camp, I took on our local university's star linebacker in a gladiatorial competition in which we attempted to knock each other off of spinning barrels with padded jousting sticks. It was all for cabin points, at least that's what we said. It didn't last long. I got hit harder than I ever have and landed harder still on the ground below. I don't think my fiancée was impressed when two weeks later I was still complaining of pain in my chest or when we found out I had broken two ribs and was instructed not to lift any luggage on our honeymoon. That wasn't how it played out in my head. I bet you have stories of your own.

Cultures of the world are filled with these feats of bravery by which men have long sought to prove themselves and mark their transition into adulthood. Often these tests form rites of passage by which young boys are welcomed into the community as men. In these cultures, maturity is awarded through the passing of a test, usually by means of pain, endurance, and self-determination. If you visit Vanuatu today, you can still witness young men jumping from those wooden towers. It has mostly become a tourist trap, with money replacing honor, but the questions those ancient men sought to answer still remain and I'm guessing after the crowds have left, the modern performers still think about it and compete for it too.

It's interesting that no comparable rite of passage is recorded among the ancient Israelites. Circumcision marked males as participants in the community of God's people, but circumcision was usually carried out just a few days after birth. The Bible doesn't record any ceremony or test by which manhood was proven.

Many modern Jews mark a boy's coming of age through the Bar Mitzvah ceremony. Unlike the feats of pain-filled endurance common in other cultures, a Bar Mitzvah records the passing of moral responsibility from a father to his son. At age thirteen, a Jewish boy becomes responsible for his own moral conduct. Up until that age, responsibility had been his father's.

Bar Mitzvah literally means "son of the commandment." A Jewish boy becomes responsible—a son—to the law. Traditionally, a boy marks that occasion by reading from the Torah and by a prayer in which his father acknowledges the passing of responsibility from himself to his son. "Blessed be He who has released me from being punishable for this boy," the father prays. Now publicly acknowledged as a full male participant in the community, the boy takes responsibility for his own sins. He does not prove himself a man; instead, he takes on the moral work of being one.

That transition into manhood is one of potential. It is not a badge he displays but a task to which he submits himself. His transition into manhood is one of accountability and submission to God. He takes on the work of self-awareness and personal attentiveness.

> We are experts at what is wrong with the world and amateurs at what is wrong with ourselves.

Why is it that as men we are often reluctant to take on that responsibility? Why is it we prefer an external test of courage to the internal work of self-awareness? I know many men who would prefer to leap from towers than risk the vulnerability of introspection and honesty. As the novelist Flannery O'Connor put it, "It's easier to bleed than sweat."[3]

We want desperately to be recognized as men, but we are slow and often unwilling to take on the hard work of knowing our own hearts and bearing the responsibility of our own wayward interests. There is always something to blame. Always an excuse. Always a dismissive wisecrack. We are experts at what is wrong with the world and amateurs at what is wrong with ourselves.

Spiritual maturity is not a natural masculine instinct. There is no instinct for self-awareness. There is no instinct for facing our sins or for bearing moral responsibility either. As an adolescent growing into adulthood, you may wake up to discover that first hair on your upper lip, but you never wake up to discover wisdom grown overnight.

Instead, maturity takes time and the growing pains of failure, correction, repentance, and transformed desire. Maturity always hurts. Growth requires pain. Oswald Chambers thus concluded, "The entrance into the kingdom of God is through the sharp, sudden pains of repentance."[4] And Chambers pointed out past generations of men "used to pray for 'the gift of tears'"[5] to find it.

CAIN'S INVITATION TO MATURITY

Cain was the firstborn of humanity. God had created his parents miraculously from the ground and from a rib, but he was the natural offspring of their union. Eve couldn't help but remark at the miracle of life from her own body. Holding her infant son, she exclaimed, "I have gotten a man with the help of the LORD" (Gen. 4:1). She named him Cain. It is a play on the Hebrew word for creating. As the translator Robert Alter explained, "Eve, upon bringing forth the third human being, imagines herself as a kind of partner of God in man-making."[6] Eve recognized that this infant man was now her responsibility. Helpless and dependent, he was hers to care for.

Not long after Cain's birth, Adam and Even welcomed a second son, Abel. As every parent I know seems to universally acknowledge, those days of childhood innocence are gone far too quickly. Before long, the two boys were men, each taking on vocations and lives of their own. Cain became a gardener and Abel a shepherd. As the seasons changed, each brought an offering to the Lord.

Their offerings marked an important passage, a passage by which the divine relationship, possessed previously by their parents, became their own. This coming of age was depicted as each took up the act of worship for himself—each with his own unique gift to offer God.

We are surprised to read that while Abel's gift was received with approval, God had no regard for Cain's. We aren't told how Cain became aware of God's rejection, but Cain knew. He became angry and frustrated. Why was his gift rejected and his brother's received? Cain wasn't the only one without an answer to that question. The question has long plagued readers and commentators alike. You can find all kinds of theories, attempted explanations, and hidden motives between the lines, but the simple answer is, we aren't told why God rejected Cain's gift. Cain didn't seem to know why either.

It's easy to read God's choice of Abel over Cain as a kind of divine favoritism. Did God just like Abel more? Isn't God supposed to be impartial? For as many times as readers have asked, surprisingly "why" is a question Cain never seems to ask. Cain was not drawn into deeper investigation of God's ways; instead, he turned his back on God in bitterness. Cain was immediately suspicious and frustrated and without response. He indulged what he felt with little consideration of any alternative explanation. As Proverbs 14:12 puts it, "There is a way that seems right to a man, but its end is the way to death."

As God had done with Adam and Eve, searching them out in their sinful hiding, now too God came to the frustrated firstborn of man and again initiated a critical conversation. "Why are you angry, and why has your face fallen? If you do well, will you not be accepted? And if you do not do well, sin is crouching at the door. Its desire is contrary to you, but you must rule over it" (Gen. 4:6–7).

That is the first mention of sin in the Bible. Adam and Eve had sinned. But it had been the external temptation of the serpent that drew Eve into disobedience. Now God spoke of it as a warning to the immature Cain, naive to the forces at work within him. Sin was crouching like a wild animal at his tent door. It sought to destroy him. He must learn to rule over it, to recognize it, and take control of it before it devoured him.

Unlike Eve's external temptation by the serpent, Cain's first encounter with sin was a blind spot in his own soul and an immaturity that couldn't recognize its risk. Reluctant and irritated, his immaturity left him gravely vulnerable. Cain was already a man by stature, but this moment was his test, a rite of passage. Could he recognize it and the lesson at hand? Could he show himself mature?

God's rejection of Cain's gift is really an opportunity. It was an opportunity for Cain to inquire more about God's ways and to understand the complexity of his own instincts and vulnerability to sin. If God had simply accepted Cain's gift, what motive would Cain have had for anything deeper than that external act of religious practice? God was after more. Cain was capable of more. This was his moment of moral discovery. God was not Cain's judge but his tutor toward a better way. This was not divine favoritism but divine instruction. God was offering Cain a lesson in maturity.

I remember one summer when my dad offered me a lesson on how to hit a curveball. He had been a great baseball player, and I was struggling. "It's going to look like it's coming in at you," he said, "but stay in there and keep your eye on it. Pick up the spin." I stayed in the box, never saw any spin, and it hit me hard in the leg. "That's what a curveball doesn't look like," he tried to explain. I'm not sure the lesson helped.

A good coach does, though, intentionally inflict challenge and pain in a controlled way. Exercise, drills, and practice are supposed to be hard and to hurt. They give us an opportunity to develop the muscles and mentality necessary for what's to come. A drill instructor may not seem like your friend, but the instructor's tenacity and aggression might one day save your life. The lesson is hard, but the wisdom it offers is invaluable. You are challenged for your own good. Those who hope to avoid the offense never learn the lesson.

Cain was welcomed into that divine conversation—an offense created by God's grace for his maturing. God wounded him for the sake of saving him. He would not allow Cain to live in the naive world of inherited faith or immature self-interest. To become a man in the space of this broken and sinful world was to face reality and the forces at work within himself. God would force Cain to see the animal stalking in his shadow. He would force Cain to take sin seriously.

It was Cain's rite of passage. His Bar Mitzvah—his becoming no longer just a son of Eve, but a son under the instruction of God. This was his moment of growth, painful but divinely offered. We have nothing recorded of Cain's response. Silence. To Cain, any question was a threat. Or as commentator James Boice explained, "One of the clearest marks of sin is our almost innate desire to excuse ourselves and complain if we are judged in any way."[7]

Without grasping your actual need, every divine gift feels like condemnation. To you, God's help is always judgment. Cain ignored the lesson and instead indulged the anger he felt. He opened the door to the sin crouching outside. He rose up against his brother and murdered him. Do not underestimate the stakes of God's lessons nor the consequence of forging your own way. Unfortunately, it is precisely this rejection of God's instruction that men are being taught to indulge.

"MEN WITHOUT CHESTS"

In 1943, C. S. Lewis published *The Abolition of Man*. Lewis was concerned about how students were being taught to think about morality—discerning right and wrong. The educational trend of his day was to show how all moral conclusions were largely expressions of individual preference. There was no right or wrong, only an individual's feeling about what is good and bad. Lewis recognized the way in which students were being taught to ascribe value to what they felt while rejecting any inherent or absolute value. This indulgence in feelings as truth makes growing beyond what you feel unobtainable. It makes recognizing your own inadequacy impossible, for they are no longer inadequacies but personal perspectives and individual truths. We are robbed of the means by which previous generations of men were helped to navigate and mature their instincts.

Lewis wrote, "Aristotle says that the aim of education is to make the pupil like and dislike what he ought."[8] Lewis agreed and understood that a moral sense of right and wrong must be taught and that, by either intentional manipulation or unintentional neglect, the skills by which we have long taught men moral maturity could be lost. He recognized that students would naturally extend this lesson to the highest authorities. They would come to trust only their personal preference and impulse.

This is the great irony I see in our current conversation with men. We have lost those ancient ways by which we taught men to like and dislike what they ought—not a question of hobbies or recreation, but of morality and purpose. We have lost the path by which we lead men to become better. We have demanded proper behavior while laughing at the idea of morality. We became experts at deconstructing moral responsibility, feeling "pleasure in [our] own knowingness."[9] We roll our eyes when others talk of virtue, character, and honor. How naive. How old-fashioned. Yet, we expect men to possess those very traits we now call out-of-date. We teach them to indulge what they feel and expect them to somehow rise above it. Where

> **Men do not lack ideals. Talk to even the most disillusioned man, and you'll find he at least once believed in the possibility of something better.**

students are taught to question the existence of goodness, they soon possess none of it and eventually lose the path altogether.

Lewis ultimately concluded: "Such is the tragi-comedy of our situation—we continue to clamour for those very qualities we are rendering impossible. . . . In a sort of ghastly simplicity we remove the organ and demand the function. We make men without chests and expect of them virtue and enterprise. We laugh at honour and are shocked to find traitors in our midst. We castrate and bid the geldings be fruitful."[10] We have become these men without chests. We are men with heads full of knowledge and stomachs growling with hunger. Yet we are without the moral maturity to rule either.

Men do not lack ideals. Talk to even the most disillusioned man, and you'll find he at least once believed in the possibility of something better. A man's disillusionment only highlights how much he really did once believe. Even Cain could imagine the possibility of true worship; what he couldn't bear was the pain necessary to better understand what true worship required of him. What men lack is an ear tuned to the divine lesson. If there is no divine prodding toward something better, we are quickly stunted in our growth and trapped by our own evaluations.

As Thomas Merton wrote, "That world was the picture of Hell, full of men like myself, loving God and yet hating Him; born to love Him, living instead in fear and hopeless self-contradictory hungers."[11]

We reap what we have sown, a wasteland of immature, chestless men. A wasteland dotted with Photoshopped billboards of masculine ideals, taunting the men who wander the pathless horizon, unable to mature beyond the growling of their stomachs. Leave this man to wander the desert long without a guide or map, and a deep disillusionment sets in. It is all a joke. Men eventually stop searching for the path. They come to despise the idea altogether. Their morality becomes selfish, pragmatic, and nihilistic. And why not? They become more animal than man, hyenas laughing at what they once believed in. A dark sarcasm creeps in; it is a front for our disdain of the world and of God. We hate what we feel but know no other way than to indulge it. We give in to the animal crouched at our tent door.

The New Testament writer Jude warned of the dangers of living in this ignorance. He criticized those who "blaspheme all that they do not understand, and they are destroyed by all that they, like unreasoning animals, understand instinctively" (v. 10). Jude recognized men in his own day who acted more like animals than men, immaturely indulging their instincts and defending their own ignorance. Jude went on to warn, "Woe to them! For they walked in the way of Cain" (v. 11). He recognized in their immaturity the same grave mistake Cain made. For Jude, this way of Cain was marked by a refusal to learn and a trusting in what we instinctively feel, like animals, acting without moral reason or clarity.

Unmoved by the divine warning, we are left with only our instincts to guide us. We make our offering and refuse to go any deeper. We mature in stature and reputation, careers and bank accounts, but inside we stay the same—moral adolescents, juvenile in our indulgence of every emotion.

Maturity does not mean you are everything you could be; instead, maturity begins by taking responsibility for who you are now, submitting to the divine lesson at hand, and humbly seeking a path toward something better.

So, how do you develop a chest? Your chest is a moral muscle which must be grown. As a boy's physical body matures into

THE 5 MASCULINE INSTINCTS

ngth, so too must his faith and morality. Recognize your weakness, isolate that muscle, and begin your reps. Admit you are not as strong as you imagine, and recognize it will require some pain to get you there. The first pains of growing are always humility and meekness. It is always humility and meekness that lead to true maturity and strength, but maybe not in the way you've previously thought of them.

HUMILITY, THE FIRST PAIN OF MATURITY

The story goes that a British newspaper once posed the question, "What's wrong with the world?" It was early in the twentieth century. The optimism of the Industrial Revolution and the scientific potential of man's progress had been shattered by the blood-soaked trenches of the First World War. Men gassed, burned, and mowed down by machine guns. Sickness, poverty, rising totalitarianism, and the collapse of reason had darkened the dawning of a century once exuberant in hope and expectation. I'm sure the newspaper was expecting thoughtful essays on how so much had gone wrong. Political evaluations, suggestions for necessary societal reform, scientific explorations—there were so many ways to approach the question. What they didn't expect was G. K. Chesterton's answer.

A prolific thinker and writer of his time, Chesterton formally submitted his own evaluation. What's wrong with the world? He wrote:

Dear Sir:
I am.
Yours,
G. K. Chesterton.[12]

It's hard to imagine Cain making such a statement. Or, if I'm being honest, me. So too, in our world of hot takes and online debate, it's hard to imagine most of us making it. Give a man a blank slate to complain and rarely will he write of his own wrong. But Chesterton was right: what's wrong with the world is me. It takes a remarkable level of maturity to recognize that, that everything wrong in the whole is also present in me. I need not commit every possible sin to share in the broken hopelessness of humanity. No one is righteous. No one seeks God. All have gone astray.

As Jesus stood on the hillside beside the Sea of Galilee, a large crowd gathered around Him. The sloping landscape provided natural amplification for His sermon. It was one of His first public addresses. It was the beginning of His public ministry, and He began by laying out a set of values that characterized the kingdom He was establishing. Many had gathered, having heard of His miracles. Rumors that He might be the long-awaited Messiah must have been quietly spreading through homes and villages. Could He be the one to overthrow Rome? Could He be the one to establish a new divine rule? Might this finally be the beginning of something better?

Jesus began:

> Blessed are the poor in spirit, for theirs is the kingdom of heaven.
> Blessed are those who mourn, for they shall be comforted.
> Blessed are the meek, for they shall inherit the earth.
> Blessed are those who hunger and thirst for righteousness, for they shall be satisfied. (Matt. 5:2–6)

Eugene Peterson tried in his Message paraphrase to translate that word "lucky." "You're lucky when you're at the end of your rope." His editor objected, and they went with the more traditional "blessed,"[13] but I've always liked Peterson's expression better. It catches the oddity of what Jesus was saying. It captures the contrast, which surely left many scratching their heads that day beside the Sea of Galilee.

Jesus' kingdom did not begin with demonstrations of political or military power. Instead, Jesus aligned Himself with the poor, the hungry, and the meek. He called them lucky. The kingdom of God belongs to those who embrace with humility their own spiritual poverty. To be poor in spirit is to grasp your fundamental need. You are not alright. You're lucky if you can recognize it.

The Greek philosopher Socrates explained, "The only true wisdom is in knowing you know nothing."[14] Jesus' emphasis on spiritual poverty is close to Socrates's, but humility is something more than acknowledged ignorance. Humility senses opportunity beyond yourself. It recognizes the value of an authority higher than yourself. We learn to fear the Lord. We learn to respect those lessons God is offering us. Fear is the beginning of wisdom. Respect is the beginning of maturity.

> In a world obsessed with self-esteem and self-expression, Christians embrace a unique form of self-suspicion. We recognize we can't trust ourselves.

Augustine once wrote to a friend, "I wish you to submit with complete devotion, and to construct no other way for yourself of grasping and holding the truth than the way constructed by Him who, as God, saw how faltering were our steps. This way is first humility, second humility, third humility, and however often you should ask me I would say the same."[15]

We often think of humility as the absence of pride. Rid yourself of pride, and you must be a humble person. As long as you aren't bragging, you must be doing a pretty good job. But humility is not passive. It takes work. It takes an active suspicion of our own motives and desires.

In a world obsessed with self-esteem and self-expression, Christians embrace a unique form of self-suspicion. We recognize we can't trust ourselves. Your first thought is not always right. Your self-evaluations are often wrong. Your instincts are prone to disaster. What you feel cannot always be trusted. The humble are suspicious of their first instinct. Where pride tends towards confidence, humility allows us to entertain the idea that we are poor, both in our capabilities and in our own self-evaluations. And so, it is this possibility of being wrong that, when embraced, opens the door to growing beyond yourself. The first pain of maturity is the pain of recognizing your own inadequacy.

You have to recognize you are in need before you are willing to learn. Cain could not grasp that fundamental need. He was unable to learn because of it. His emotions insisted that he had been wronged, that it was all a threat to his well-being. Without this self-suspicion, he was incapable of receiving the divine lesson; he couldn't recognize he needed it. Without self-suspicion, every divine word becomes a threat to your carefully constructed defense.

In the field of psychology, there is a bias known as the Dunning-Kruger effect. Researchers have consistently demonstrated that humans tend to overestimate their abilities and skills. When researchers tested participants in areas such as grammar and logic, they found that, though many scored as low as the twelfth percentile, they routinely self-estimated that they had scored as high as the sixty-second percentile.[16]

In another experiment, researchers asked participants if they were familiar with a series of topics related to politics, biology, physics, and geography. What they didn't tell participants was that the researchers had inserted entirely made-up topics alongside real ones. Ninety percent of participants claimed to have some knowledge of the made-up terms.

It gets worse. This bias seems to be stronger in men. One study found that while only thirty-three percent of female students thought they were smarter than the class average, sixty-six percent of men thought they were.[17] That math doesn't work—sixty-six percent can't be above their own class average. Obviously, someone was wrong about themselves. Many had overestimated their own ability.

David Dunning explained, "Incompetent people do not recognize—scratch that, cannot recognize—just how incompetent they are. . . . In many cases, incompetence does not leave people disoriented, perplexed, or cautious. Instead, the incompetent are often blessed with an inappropriate confidence, buoyed by *something* that feels to them like knowledge."[18] It's as dangerous as it sounds. Our ignorance actually keeps us from recognizing we are ignorant. Our ignorance can feel like knowledge. Our ignorance can create confidence.

The Bible has long warned us of this tendency. What is so insidious about pride and our self-confidence is that it loves to leverage the success of our good deeds to keep us dumb. There is a way of worship that keeps you in control and blocks the work of God. As Cain made his offering, so we too worship and tithe, the pride we feel at our proper participation blocking us from recognizing the need for anything more. Cloaked in the appearance of morality, we feel no pressure to question it. Our religious deeds become an excuse for shutting down our minds and coasting. It's why Augustine was so adamant about humility. "If you should ask, and as often as you should ask, about the precepts of the Christian religion, my inclination would be to answer nothing but humility."[19] The moment you lose sense of your need, you have wandered off the path.

Jewish teachers often turn to humor to show the irony of this point. As they tell it, one day during synagogue the rabbi was overcome with a sense of God's presence and holiness. Deeply moved, he unexpectedly cried out, "Lord, I am nothing!" and fell to the ground. Not wanting to appear less religious, the cantor likewise cried out, "Lord, I am nothing!" and fell down beside the rabbi. At the back of the room was a poor handyman who occasionally worked on things around the synagogue. Likewise, he too cried out, "Lord, I am nothing!" and fell down as well. The rabbi nudged the cantor lying beside him and whispered, "Look who thinks he's nothing!"

> I routinely find that God asks far less of us than we realize. What He asks for is a humble recognition of our need.

Humility is not God's goal to grind you into the ground, to rub your insufficiencies in your face; rather, He can do nothing good in your life unless you are willing to recognize your need for it. It is man's indifference and pride that keeps him from God, not his shortcomings. God was not asking Cain for anything more than attention and the humility to wonder what might be going on. He wanted only enough self-suspicion to free Cain from his own instincts and turn his attention toward God and possibilities beyond himself.

But Cain's face was downcast as if he could not look beyond himself. Pride always keeps us nearsighted. It is only the humble desperation of need that allows us to look up from the smallness of our own insecurities to something more.

John Calvin wrote near the beginning of his *Institutes of the Christian Religion*: "It is evident that man never attains to a true self-knowledge until he has previously contemplated the face of God, and come down after such contemplation to look into himself. For (such is our innate pride) we always seem to ourselves just, and upright, and wise, and holy, until we are convinced, by clear evidence, of our injustice, vileness, folly, and impurity."[20]

I routinely find that God asks far less of us than we realize. What He asks for is a humble recognition of our need. Blessed are those who hunger and thirst, for they will be satisfied. Blessed are those who are willing to identify with their spiritual poverty, for they are His kingdom. Lucky are those who realize they are often wrong. They're lucky because that realization is the path beyond yourself and toward God.

MEEKNESS, THE SECOND PAIN OF MATURITY

My wife comes from a family of girls—three daughters. They still joke and tease one another about arguments they had as kids. My favorite of those stories was the time my wife's younger sister refused to help her clean up toys on the stairs, sarcastically taunting her to "do it yourself." My wife grabbed the nearby vacuum and stuck it to the side of her sister's head. The roller tangled in her hair and ripped out a patch of it, leaving a bald spot for the whole school year. My wife insists I let you know how bad she still feels about that childish decision.

You don't have to teach kids to react to perceived wrongs. It comes most naturally. It is Newton's third law of motion: "For every action, there is an equal and opposite reaction." In humans, I've found the reaction is not always equal to the action. The toddler whose toy is stolen finds it most natural to strike back and often elevate the offense. Adults become craftier in their revenge, but usually the impulse is the same. When we are punched, we punch back. It is a sign of our enslavement to instinct. Unable to question our impulses and overconfident in our perceptions, we are quick to react.

Don't you see it in Cain's violent response? What drove Cain to action was reaction. He couldn't not respond. Offended by God, he reacted, taking it out on his brother. Refusing God's lesson, he acted by his own logic. If you want to understand the logic by which you live, look no further than how you react.

Humility can seem abstract and theoretical. There's no assessment for scoring or tracking your progress, and as many wise believers have pointed out, if you pay too much attention to your own humility, it has a tendency to turn bad on you. Instead, I would recommend you give greater attention to the virtue of meekness.

Meekness is always a test of reaction. I consider it to be one of the most neglected and yet important masculine virtues. I would go so far as to say that not much else in this book will matter without this first virtue. You fail to learn the lessons of humility and meekness, and all other moral achievements will be only food for pride's feasting.

If sarcasm is a sign of avoiding God's lesson of maturity, then humility is a self-suspicion by which we become open to questioning our instincts, and meekness the practice of suspecting our impulse to act. It is a way of freeing ourselves from the immaturity of reaction.

Our culture has trained us to pay very little attention to meekness. It gets some vague sense of approval for Jesus including it in His Beatitudes, but no one is talking or thinking about meekness—not in this world. A politician or leader might be happy to have a reputation for humility but would never want the label of being meek. How would you feel if someone commented about you, "You're just such a meek person"? Could you even conclude they meant it as a compliment? And whatever Jesus meant by "the meek shall inherit the earth," it's hard to see much evidence of that.

The German philosopher Nietzsche saw meekness as a Christian pollutant, hindering the progress of man. Nietzsche saw modern man's rejection of God as an opportunity to form a new stronger humanity. From Nietzsche's perspective, the constraint meekness imposed on man's ambition held him back. Virtues like meekness kept a man from asserting the full potential of his control. Derek Rishmawy explains that Nietzsche "thought meekness was exactly the sort of false virtue that the weak would applaud because, well, it's about the only virtue they could actually pull off."[21]

Nietzsche's evaluation of meekness sounds very modern. We suspect it is a virtue weak men claim to justify their weakness. But many ancient writers were more positive about meekness. Plato used the word to describe a general who, victorious in battle, was put in a position of ultimate power.[22] He was justified in annihilating his enemy, but Plato called the general who instead spared the conquered people meek in his treatment. Plato saw that not as a weakness but strength—an inner control.

Similarly, the Greek philosopher and soldier Xenophon often used the word meek in his description of war horses.[23] The best horses would be tamed but not broken of their spirit. A horse prepared for battle would need to maintain a wild nature but be brought under the control of its rider. Its nature needed to be disciplined but not forfeited. A prized warhorse still possessed all of the traits that made it wild: strength, determination, and fearlessness. It would face cannons and muskets, fire and smoke, cries and chaos. But it must also recognize and respond to the most subtle shift of its rider, the kick of a heel, the whispered command, and at its best, anticipate even before commanded.

I have a chestnut quarter horse that my family enjoys riding. He could hardly be described as a horse ready for battle. He is more pet than steed, but the willingness of an animal his size to cut in a new direction with only the slightest pressure of a knee is remarkable to me. Even after years of riding, he has not lost his personality. He is still mischievous, strong, and prone to test each new rider's limits, but once established, his obedience is remarkable. He is meek, not a statement of his weakness but of his disciplined strength.

Meekness doesn't breed out the horse's power; meekness matures it into something useful, something controllable, something disciplined, something better. A meek person can still feel that burning desire for reaction, but they have discovered their real strength lies in the discipline of being led by God, not their emotions. To put it another way, a fighter's strength is not only in his punch but also in his ability to take one. The ability to absorb the blow is also a mark of strength.

This meekness is strength without the insecurity to prove

it. It is self-control that doesn't need to be in control to feel it. So much of what appears to be power in this world is really just desperation, and so much of what appears to be strength is just flailing insecurity.

The challenge of meekness is that it cannot be manufactured by self-determination or will. The wild horse cannot tame himself. He can't even perceive the idea. He needs a higher authority. He needs a master wise enough to bring his power to heel. He needs discipline and the lesson. Meekness is first a question of submission.

Peter captured an image of Jesus' remarkable meekness in writing, "When he was reviled, he did not revile in return; when he suffered, he did not threaten." Where did such restraint and strength come from? Peter explained, Jesus "continued entrusting himself to him who judges justly" (1 Peter 2:23). Jesus' meekness was not a character trait or some innate disposition, nor was it self-determination to demonstrate virtue and show Himself to be a superior man. Jesus' meekness was a submission to God's plan. He entrusted Himself. He became "obedient to the point of death" (Phil. 2:8).

> I know you want desperately to be the lone rider, seated on your horse, determined and self-reliant as you ride westward into the setting sun. But that is not your calling. You are the horse, not the rider.

Charles Spurgeon picked up on this mystery in writing of God's patience: "'The Lord is slow to anger,' because He is great in power. He is truly great in power who hath power over himself. When God's power doth restrain Himself, then it is power indeed:

the power that binds omnipotence is omnipotence surpassed."[24]

The question of meekness is not how much of it you possess but how much of yourself you've submitted. It is this yielding to surpassing omnipotence that produces meekness. Your strength is directly related to the strength of that authority to which you are willing to submit yourself. Meekness requires a rider, a commander, an authority. It requires the humility to surrender ourselves to His leading.

I know you want desperately to be the lone rider, seated on your horse, determined and self-reliant as you ride westward into the setting sun. But that is not your calling. You are the horse, not the rider. Confident and strong only when you are ruled by one greater. Without His direction, you are an undisciplined beast, easily spooked, and wildly restless.

Our modern masculine ideal is too individualistic, too independent, and often too self-absorbed to recognize the strength of meekness. Submission is its antithesis. Submission is weakness and the forfeiting of the masculine ideal. Submission is domestic and womanish. To submit is to be broken and robbed of your masculine vitality. It's no wonder submission becomes a perverted word in our demanding of it from others. But submission is rightfully a masculine ideal. It is man's most wise move by which the strength of meekness is given room to form. It is the means by which he entrusts himself to a master and takes up the work of following and learning. It is our submission that builds strength. We must be broken, not to lose our masculine spirit but to have it matured into something stronger—something of use in this world, something of use to God.

Meekness is the bit and bridle to our headstrong arrogance and impulsive reaction. The tugged reins by which God calls for our halt and the same loosened which guide us on to better pasture. Only the man who has submitted to His lead can discern the difference. He is a horse well prepared for battle, his undisciplined brother only for paddocks. To him, the bit is an irritant and he spends his day trying to throw it.

The man who cannot be led, who submits to nothing but himself, is far weaker than the man who submits to God, and he that cannot question his own instincts is weakest of all.

THE LAND OF WANDERING

How dumb and undisciplined Cain must have sounded in his sarcastic reply to God. By his sarcasm, he made plain his lack of humility and meekness. He was a weak and immature man. He hadn't fooled anyone but himself. God responded, "The voice of your brother's blood is crying to me from the ground" (Gen. 4:10). Cain was busted. The blood of his brother spoke with greater conviction than he did. He had gotten away with nothing. God continued, "Now you are cursed from the ground, which has opened its mouth to receive your brother's blood from your hand. When you work the ground, it shall no longer yield to you its strength. You shall be a fugitive and a wanderer on the earth" (Gen. 4:11–12).

Again, God's lesson was less a curse than a statement of how things would be. These are the consequences of refusing God's lesson. These are the consequences of Cain's immaturity and prideful reaction. Isolation, loss of strength, and endless wandering are always the outcome of our refusal to submit and mature. Cain was carried away from God's presence to the land of Nod. In Hebrew, it is the place of wandering.

Cain finally buckled under God's words. He lamented, "My

punishment is greater than I can bear" (Gen. 4:13). Cain, by his immaturity, had long proved how little he could bear.

He ended up adrift—a lost boy incapable of growing up. It is sad and far, far too common. Boastful and sarcastic, too many men end up wandering that land of Nod. They are not strong but perpetually impulsive and weak. Not humble but proud. Not meek but foolhardy. Their sarcasm no longer funny. They have refused the discipline of a heavenly Father. Submitting to no one, they are cut off from all.

God has lessons before you as well. It probably won't be comfortable. There will be pain. It will cost you the naive simplicity of your youth. It will feel like a threat and often seem unfair. That may not be what you want to hear, but never mistake it for a curse. It is your cure. It is your cross. To die to self is to be given something far better and a better self along with it. As Jim Elliot famously wrote, "He is no fool who gives what he cannot keep to gain what he cannot lose."[25]

Your sarcasm will not cover you for long. But the divine lesson offers you entrance, by submission, into the fullness God created you to be: real strength, true maturity, self-suspicion, and meekness. Take the lesson. Mature into the man God is leading you to be.

* * *

Recognize your instinct for sarcasm.
Recognize your need for humility and meekness.

Chapter 4

ADVENTURE: CULTIVATING NEW EYES

THE SAMSON STORY: JUDGES 13-16

"Listen to your life. See it for the fathomless mystery it is. In the boredom and pain of it, no less than in the excitement and gladness: touch, taste, smell your way to the holy and hidden heart of it, because in the last analysis all moments are key moments, and life itself is grace."

FREDERICK BUECHNER, *Now and Then*

"At times it seems as if arranging to have no commitment of any kind to anyone would be a special freedom. But in fact the whole idea works in reverse. The most deadly commitment of all is to be committed only to one's self. Some come to realize this after they are in the nursing home."

JOHN D. MACDONALD, *The Lonely Silver Rain*

When the opening day of the Missouri turkey season happened to fall on the same day as my thirtieth birthday, I took it as a sign from God. I needed a vacation; I needed an adventure. I was four years into a church plant, two years into starting a freelance web-design business to help support that church plant, and I had just celebrated the birth of our second child. I had a partly remodeled master bath I was trying to finish, and I was working on losing a few pounds I had kept since college. In so many ways, I could recognize God's hand guiding my life, but still, I was feeling tired and wrestling with questions about the future. I took three days off work, packed my shotgun, a case of Diet Coke, a stack of frozen Mexican TV dinners, and headed to a relative's farm.

Shakespeare described man's second stage as a restless lover sighing with his woeful ballad. His restlessness was a desperation for something more, for life to finally begin in all of its anticipated excitement and adventure. A man ready to discover who he really was, adventure the path to lead him to that critical self-discovery. Surely man was made for more than cubicles and coffee breaks. It's that unsettled feeling I think many of us men live just trying to ignore.

I had my decoys out and was leaned against an old maple tree at the edge of a plowed field long before the sun rose. As usual, the field was heavy with fog. I waited until just before sunrise and made my first call of the season.

As it broke the stillness, a moment passed—silent, empty— and then, from just twenty or thirty yards behind me, a turkey let loose its booming gobble. Another answered from a few trees farther. Then the whole river bottom broke out in gobbling, six, maybe seven birds. I called again, and again they answered, this time each fighting for position in response. About that same moment, two flew down from their roost and landed seventy-five yards in front of me.

I leaned down and pressed my cheek against the stock of my shotgun, the barrel now resting on my knee. I called softly as both birds turned and began to trot toward me, stopping every few yards to gobble and fan out their feathers. I picked out the larger of the two birds and made myself wait until he was just thirty yards out. I clucked once on my call. He stopped, folded his feathers, and lifted his head in curiosity, silhouetting it against the dirt of the cut field behind him.

I centered the shotgun's bead, silently pressed off the safety, held my breath, and slowly squeezed the trigger. The muzzle flashed bright against the cool shades of dawn and the percussion echoed for miles down the river, a strange and unnatural sound. The woods went quiet. There, twenty yards from the barrel, was a trophy: a twenty-three-pound Ozark Eastern turkey. I broke open my gun, ejected the empty shell, and walked over to the bird, feeling proud and like a man. That's how it's done, I thought to myself. I've gotten pretty good at this. Then it hit me: Missouri regulations only allow for one turkey to be harvested in the first week of the season. I was done.

I looked down at my watch—6:43 a.m. What was I supposed to do with the three days I had taken off work? What was I supposed to do with all those TV dinners? Walking back to the house—the bird slung over my shoulder—I realized how fitting this moment was. This was exactly what turning thirty felt like. This was my life. I cleaned the turkey, packed my bags, made a cup of coffee, and left for home before noon. I was back changing diapers and dealing with work emails by two.

I had celebrated turning thirty with forty-five minutes of adventure.

SAMSON'S PURSUIT OF ADVENTURE

Outside the Russian Grand Palace of Peterhof sits one of the great statues of the biblical man Samson. A fountain cast in gold, it depicts a chiseled, shirtless Samson ripping apart the jaws of a roaring lion with his bare hands. Samson looks Herculean. You can almost hear the popping and cracking of the lion's jawbones buckling under Samson's strength. The whole scene is suspended in tension. Samson looks every part the hero. Like the sultriest of Greek gods, he gives form to courage and brawn. This is the kind of guy they put on the cover of Harlequins. Samson is the archetype of masculine adventure.

He is everything an adventurous man might imagine becoming: venturing into exotic new lands, battling wild beasts, wooing beautiful women, passing bottles of wine, and constantly facing danger and daring escapes. I like to imagine him in Ray-Bans, a man bun, and a CrossFit T-shirt, hiking through some remote red stone canyon, documenting his adventurous life on Instagram, National Park stickers all over the back of his dusty Land Rover. He was driven by passion and restless for romance and his next adventure.

You probably remember Samson by his hair—the supposed secret to his strength. It is an important part of his story, but maybe the more important feature was his eyes. The book of Judges tells us in the opening words of Samson's life that he *saw* a Philistine woman whom he wanted for his wife. Samson explained to his parents that "she is right in my eyes" (Judg. 14:3). It is a theme central to the book of Judges in which Samson's story is told and central to the challenge of so many growing up in that ancient Israelite culture.

The book of Judges opens where the book of Joshua left off. Israel had conquered large swaths of the promised land, but much of it remained uncontested in enemy hands. Israel began to accept a "good-enough" existence. Each tribe settled into their new land. Families went about learning the skills of farming and harvesting. Israel settled down into this new existence.

Before long, the epic storyline of Israel, formed by the luminary Moses and led through wilderness hazards by a divine pillar of fire, just kind of fizzled out. It gave way to farm chores, Philistine curiosities, and border disputes—their new life in the promised land. Each did what seemed best and necessary to himself. Doing what was right in their own eyes had less to do with failed morality than failed vision. The Israelites simply lost any conviction or sense of God working a story. Israel gave up expecting anything more.

They lost the adventure, what the author of Proverbs probably meant when he wrote, "Where there is no prophetic vision the people cast off restraint" (Prov. 29:18). Can you blame Samson for wanting a more meaningful and adventurous existence? Hadn't God called them to more than just survival? Adrift with no sense of calling or purpose, the Israelites' loss of story left them shrinking into the emptiness of a small, self-centered world, and it left them increasingly vulnerable to the seductive propaganda of Philistia.

We don't often recognize how tempting the Philistines must have been for young Israelite men like Samson. We tend to think of Israel as an advanced and sophisticated religious society and the Philistines as backward and barbaric pagans. But that's completely the opposite of what we find in the time of Samson. During the period of Judges when Samson's story was told, there wasn't even a king in Israel—not even a centralized government or place of worship. Israel was a loosely associated group of tribes scraping out an existence in the hills above the great Philistine cities. There were no great buildings or monuments. No walls, no palaces, no chariots, no ports for merchant ships, no army, no Jewish contribution to the ancient world wonders. The Israelites were just trying to learn to survive in their new homeland.

Samson had been born with the promise that he would begin a deliverance for his people. A deliverance from this small haphazard existence. But Samson was also born into one of the strictest and most peculiar Israelite customs. Most religious vows are taken voluntarily; Samson's vow wasn't. Samson was born a Nazirite. This commitment had been commanded to his parents by an angelic messenger: no wine, no contact with the dead, and no cutting his hair. It's not hard to imagine how a teenage boy might have come to see these restrictions as odd and far too limiting. His family's strange religious restrictions must have made life in Israel feel even more cramped and backward. He could imagine so much more.

On the other hand, the Philistines possessed a rich culture of progress, achievement, and a constant striving for more. They were known for their massive urban developments and their technological breakthroughs in metal. Their armies were legendary, equipped with the latest in battlefield innovation—iron—and their kings were rich beyond anything Israel had yet known. Some historians believe the Philistines migrated to Canaan from ancient Greece. They were Aegean Sea people, carried to Canaanite shores by distant trade winds, bringing with them their exotic foreign gods and fascinating cultural traditions.

Just beyond the hills of Samson's modest Israelite home lay the glistening stone walls of those Philistine cities, the deep blue haze of the Mediterranean their distant backdrop, palm trees, ocean breezes, and the faint whisper of markets bustling with merchants, travelers, wealth from all over the world, and beautiful women adorned in the latest pagan fashions. Samson's imagination painted in all the alluring details.

So, these fantasies of Philistia must have quickly invaded Samson's consciousness, a presence even when out of sight. He couldn't help himself. Story after story, Samson kept going down to their cities. Those rituals about hair and alcoholic prohibition made him all the more desperate to get out of the Israelite bubble. His heart had been captured by all things Philistine. So, his story began with his adventure to the Philistine town of Timnah, led there by his curious eyes and his hunger for something less familiar.

There is no reason to try to convince yourself that the same whirlwinds of infatuation and adventure don't tear through the boredom of your life as well. You know that subtle temptation to walk away and go looking for something more exciting—the glistening images of distant shores and fascinating new experiences. Those Philistine cities have plagued us for centuries: Shangri La, Atlantis, the Fountain of Youth, the Holy Grail, the greener grass just on the other side.

THE CALL OF ADVENTURE

Men have long sought adventure, that's nothing new. Talk of heroic quests and daring feats are as old as storytelling itself, but men today seem especially restless for it. The travel industry has reported that adventure vacations are increasing in popularity by sixty-five percent a year, making it one of the fastest-growing segments of the travel industry.[1] Relaxing by the pool or at some posh ski resort is being replaced by millennials backpacking remote South American trails, ardous expeditions to Antarctica, and selfies taken at the summit of Mount Kilimanjaro. But these adventure seekers are not just looking for an adrenaline rush or some exotic destination with picturesque scenery.

According to surveys conducted by the Adventure Travel Trade Association, the number one reason travelers sought adventure was a desire for personal transformation. It doesn't take trade surveys or a degree in psychology to recognize that man's search for adventure has always been a search for something much deeper than adrenaline.

In 1949, Joseph Campbell published *The Hero with a Thousand Faces*. Campbell was a mythologist, a 1940s Indiana Jones-type, who traveled to exotic places in those silver piston prop planes out of Casablanca. Campbell explored some of the most remote people groups of the world and collected their myths—stories about creation and struggle, the volatile temperaments of their gods, and, on occasion, the heroes who triumphed over it all. After years of collecting these stories, Campbell developed what he coined "the monomyth": the single plot encompassing all great legends across every religion and tribe.

Campbell explained, "The usual hero adventure begins with someone from whom something has been taken, or who feels there's something lacking in the normal experiences available or permitted to the members of his society. This person then takes off on a series of adventures beyond the ordinary, either to recover what has been lost or to discover some life-giving elixir."[2]

For Campbell, a hero leaves behind his common life and sets out to face challenges beyond his imagination. Facing and defeating some dragon or monster—usually a representation of facing his own fears—the hero returns home a new man. A man with a story worth telling and a newfound confidence in himself. That's the personal transformation so many adventure seekers are in pursuit of.

Campbell described this mythic story arch as the "call to adventure," and he deeply believed it continues to be the single narrative to offer meaning to individual lives today. To discover your truest self, you must find your true adventure.

Campbell wrote, "Our life has become so economic and practical in its orientation that, as you get older, the claims of the moment upon you are so great, you hardly know where . . . you are, or what it is you intended. You are always doing something that is required of you."

Campbell went on to explain, "The religious people tell us we really won't experience bliss until we die and go to heaven. But I believe in having as much as you can of this experience while you are still alive. . . . If you do follow your bliss you put yourself on a kind of track that has been there all the while, waiting for you, and the life that you ought to be living is the one you are living. I say, follow your bliss and don't be afraid."[3]

You may never have heard of Joseph Campbell, but you have been given that advice before:

"Follow your dreams."
"Do what you love, and you'll never work a day in your life."
"Life is short; make every moment count."

Don't you hear adventure calling? Take up your sword. Face your dragons. Discover something more than this mediocre life. You weren't made to live in that cubicle. Why not set out to discover who you really are, who you were meant to be?

I want adventure just as much as everyone else seems to. Exploring my own desires, the inspiration to chase new dreams, permission to throw out others' expectations, to become who I most want to be. The idea of venturing off in pursuit of bliss sounds so compelling, but is your bliss actually that easy to follow? Is it even an adventure if you get to plan it?

Samson's story is not just about a foolish man who gave up

the secret to his supernatural powers. Samson's story is about the realization that your heart's desires and your instinct for adventure will eventually betray you. Your adventures don't turn out to be that adventurous.

Adventure is a compelling instinct, but what we actually experience is explained much better by Francis Spufford: "You glimpse an unflattering vision of yourself as a being whose wants make no sense, don't harmonize: whose desires, deep down, are discordantly arranged, so that you truly want to possess and you truly want not to, at the very same time. You're equipped, you realize, for farce (or even tragedy) more than you are for happy endings."[4] This is the lesson of Samson's tragic life.

WASTED ON A DRUNKEN PUN

Though born into the Nazirite way of life, you can read Samson's story as a series of adventure stories—led by his undiscerning passions and desires—which systematically challenged each of those Nazirite commitments: No touching a corpse, no alcohol, and no cutting his hair. It is a story of passionate self-pursuit set against the nagging restraint of commitment.

Those challenges began as Samson traveled with his parents to Timnah to arrange his marriage to the Philistine girl who had caught his eye. At some point, while separated from his parents and walking through the vineyards outside of town, a lion came roaring upon him. He had no weapon for self-defense, but, at that moment, the Spirit of the Lord came upon him as he ripped the lion into pieces with his bare hands. The author of Judges tells us that Samson tore the lion apart like a young goat. It was a miracle.

It was Samson's first realization of his hallmark strength—the characteristic that has marked his life throughout history. The story reverberates with typical Samson sensuality. The muscles tightening in his body. The adrenaline coursing through his veins. His eyes straining for their target. Sweat cast across his brow. The lion's roar breaking through the grapevines. Flashing glimpses of teeth set open like a trap. And then the moment of impact and the buckling of the animal's body under Samson's resistance. It was a moment of divine clarity—a revelation. An adventurous burst of energy in an otherwise banal existence. One day strange, the next, strong. But not just strong like any other man, this was heroic strength, strength of a divine proportion. Samson must have known the prophecies about his deliverance. Might this be the beginning of something better?

The next time Samson passed through those vineyards he couldn't help stopping to look at the lion's carcass. His curiosity had him wanting another taste of that momentary thrill. If his first encounter with the lion had been self-defining, the second was an opportunity for an even greater revelation. Turning back to where he had killed the lion, Samson found its rotting corpse, but, as he came closer, there was a new sound: buzzing. Leaning down for a closer look, Samson discovered a swarm of bees had built a hive in the lion's carcass. The hive was now oozing with warm, golden honey.

That is not a natural sight. Bees do not live in rotting flesh along with maggots and flies. Only on rare occasions would they take up residence in a dried carcass. It was not what Samson had expected to find. It made no sense. The sound of the bees, the smell of rotting flesh, the image of the hive waxed into the lion's ribs, the taste of honey on his tongue, the feeling of it scraped out into his hands. What did it mean? There was nothing Samson could make sense of. Whatever Samson had hoped to find in returning, this wasn't it. Samson must have been puzzled by it, but not for too long. He was on his way to a girl in Timnah. We read, "He scraped it out into his hands and went on, eating as he went" (Judg. 14:9).

> Samson's tendency was to exchange these mysteries of God's leading for a cheap self-indulgence. He simply lacked the discernment to sense what he was actually in on, the better adventure already underway.

The Hebrew uses an interesting set of words to describe the lion and the bees. It could be translated that Samson found, in the *ruin* of the lion, a *congregation* of bees. Could it be an experience by which Samson could see his own destiny, that in the ruin of the Philistines, the congregation of Israel would find a place of peace, a land flowing with honey? Was it Samson's place to use this new divine strength to bring about the Philistine ruin as he had the lion's?

Samson never seems to have recognized that it was the Spirit who had gifted him with strength that day or that it was God who had placed that peculiar image in his path. He had no time for the discernment such puzzles might require. Infatuated by his own conception of calling and adventure, he took the honey for himself and went on his way.

Instead, Samson did what would become characteristic of his life: he turned the whole experience into his own game, a drunken riddle gambled away at his wedding feast. Samson's tendency was to exchange these mysteries of God's leading for a cheap self-indulgence. He simply lacked the discernment to sense what he was actually in on, the better adventure already underway. Maybe worse, having used his own hand to scrape the honey out of the lion's corpse, Samson seemed ambivalent to having broken his Nazirite vow. That too was a characteristic that would continue.

A wedding in the ancient world was usually celebrated with several days of partying and drinking. In the original Hebrew, the description of Samson's wedding is painted with innuendoes of drunkenness and yet another forfeited vow. As entertainment, the men began to gamble on riddles. The lion was still on his mind. No one would guess something so strange. "Out of the eater came something to eat. Out of the strong came something sweet" (Judg. 14:14). His Philistine partiers had seven days to solve it. For thirty garments as the prize, Samson had sold away his experience as a game.

There is a commandment against taking the Lord's name in vain; it should apply to His divine experiences too. The roar of lions traded for the chatter of inebriated Philistines. The buzzing of bees for a cheap turn of phrase. The rich savoring of honey—mystery—for bottom-shelf wine fit for the end of the party. All of it was in poor taste, shallow, and small-minded.

The Philistines eventually answered Samson with, "What is sweeter than honey? What is stronger than a lion?" (Judg. 14:18). It was a riddle in reverse. It solved Samson's—a lion and honey—but it also posed the answer as yet another. They were pointing to the Philistine girl Samson had taken as a bride, the one who had betrayed him by giving away the answer. She was the thing stronger than the lion and sweeter than the honey. His desire for her had done what the lion couldn't: beaten him.

That cycle played out over and over in Samson's story. A

desire would call him away from home into his next adventure; he would find himself in trouble; the spirit would rescue him through miraculous strength; and Samson would turn it into another pun, another game, another self-indulgent boast. His adventures became smaller and increasingly self-obsessed.

A lion's corpse, a donkey's jawbone, vineyards in Timnah and Sorek, a drunken feast with Philistines, prostitutes, violence, and finally that fateful night in which Samson trusted his greatest secret to Delilah. With each adventure, the commitment to his Nazirite vow grew weaker. Samson was never transformed into something more. His restlessness never faded. He was pushed further and further from home, from his commitments, from his God.

FORCING THE QUESTION OF COMMITMENT

Is there any adventure greater than love? All the great adventure stories include it: from D'Artagnan's love for Constance to Odysseus's longing to return to Penelope. For how often the Bible speaks of relationships and marriage, it is surprising how rarely this romantic love is mentioned. Characters marry, but rarely does the Bible describe them as in love. Samson is a rare exception. We are explicitly told that Samson was in love with Delilah. For the first time, the world was bigger than himself.

Though she played the part, she was never really in love with him. The Philistine kings had offered Delilah a great sum of money to seduce Samson and uncover the secret to his strength. Three times she pressed Samson for his secret, and three times he gave her half-truths. First, he told her that if he were bound with fresh bowstrings, he would be like any other man. Delilah did just what Samson had described. Once he was bound, she shouted, "The Philistines are upon you, Samson!" (Judg. 16:9). Philistine assassins, hiding in the shadows, rushed to seize him. But Samson snapped the strings and defeated his attackers.

The story played out just the same two more times. First, it was bowstrings. Then, it was new ropes. Finally, his hair was braided. Each time assassins would pounce, and each time Samson would break free and deliver himself. The first time he shared his secret with Delilah, Samson might have rationalized the attack as a coincidence, but, after three times, it's hard to see Delilah's actions as anything other than betrayal. Samson had to have realized she was in on the setup. But remarkably, he kept playing her game.

Why continue to love and toy with a woman determined to kill you? Here is where your honesty is most needed. Is Samson's dangerous game of love, sex, and betrayal all that different than your own infatuations and temptations for romance and adventure? Do you not see how your own commitments are sacrificed for the sake of one more thrill, one more night of indulgence, one more taste of adventure?

Be it sex or a search for distant shores, our wandering so often costs us everything we had once committed ourselves to. We give it all up. When it comes to adventure, the danger often serves only to heighten the attraction. We think we have only shared half-truths and will walk away unscathed. I don't think Samson's actions are actually all that unusual.

You probably remember the story as Delilah tricking Samson into telling her his secret, but that isn't actually what Scripture says. After failing to get the secret, Delilah pressed deeper. She said to him, "'How can you say, 'I love you,' when your heart is not with me? You have mocked me these three times, and you have not told me where your great strength lies.' And when she pressed him hard with her words day after day, and urged him, his soul was vexed to death. And he told her all his heart" (Judg. 16:15–17).

She pressed him for intimacy—for commitment. She went after his heart. She wanted his secret as a sign of his commitment to her and to love. No matter how far he wandered, commitment was not ultimately a question he could avoid. Life always forces the question of commitment.

He told her more than a secret; Samson told her all his heart. His words were finally honest, for the first time, no longer another riddle. He told her everything. Samson explained that he was a Nazirite, dedicated to God since his birth. He explained to Delilah his calling and commitments. He explained his hair was the secret symbol of that commitment. As he put it, "If my head is shaved, then my strength will leave me, and I shall become weak and be like any other man" (Judg. 16:17).

It had nothing to do with magical hair. As it had always been, his hair was nothing more than the symbolic image of his heart and his commitment to God. The uncut hair was his commitment to a growing interior life, a commitment to the unique work God wanted to do in and through him. He laid that life down before Delilah. He gave up believing by faith and offered himself to what he could feel.

This moment of pleasure and vulnerability was his reality—this was his hope. He had spent his life trusting his first instinct to leave, to go, to abandon the ordinary in pursuit of the exotic. That life of leaving had not made him wiser, nor had all those adventurous experiences transformed him into a person of character. His experiences hadn't helped him better understand the world; he now seemed to understand it less. He was left desperate, lonely, and undiscerning. His unchecked instinct for adventure demanded the severing of that final thread of commitment.

The final words of his confession hung in midair with a kind of poetic weight, more being said than the words spoken. Cut his hair, and he would be "like any other man." That confession echoes with the sounds of longing. The sex, the adventure, the conflict, and competition had all been attempts to find what everyone else seemed to have, to be like every other man. Don't you know what Samson was describing? Do you not find yourself wishing and searching for the same?

I can't prove it, but I think Samson may have allowed Delilah to shave off his hair as he slept in her lap. He was done, done with any commitment to people or God. He was tired of the games. Tired of the searching. Tired of the adventure. He would have her or nothing.

So, Samson fell asleep on Delilah's lap. Samson finally came to rest. It wouldn't last.

BETRAYING YOURSELF

Delilah betrayed him again. After shaving his head, she called out once more, "Samson, the Philistines are upon you!" Samson attempted another defense and was crushed with a new realization: "He did not know that the LORD had left him" (Judg. 16:20). His strength was gone.

Without the Lord, there was no power. As the Philistines seized him, there was no fight left in him. Samson was gone—alive but drained of his holy zeal. He was like every other man. The consequences were devastating. The Philistines gouged his eyes. They dragged him deep into enemy territory. They bound his hands in bronze shackles. They forced him to grind wheat at the mill in their prison. They mocked him and ridiculed him for entertainment.

But Delilah's betrayal served only to visualize Samson's self-betrayal. Samson reaped the life he had sown. Samson had given his life to what he saw, doing what was right in his own eyes. He was now blinded by it. His sight had betrayed him. Samson had lived for the pursuit of adventure, the thrill of new places. Now, he was chained to a prison wall. His strength, the great mark of his identity, had betrayed him. He now worked grinding wheat at a Philistine mill. His vocation had betrayed him. No one came to his rescue. His own people betrayed him. His only love cast him aside for common coins. Sex and romance had betrayed him. Everything Samson had ever pursued had been a lie, a self-betrayal. What had come of all his feats? As W. B. Yeats wrote, "Life seems to me a preparation for something that never happens."[5] Samson's adventure was over. He was not a deliverer but just like every other Israelite. The greater story of God lost in pursuit of their own.

The miraculous gift of God's calling and purpose disintegrated into this: a blind prisoner, shackled and enslaved. The path of self-pursuit always leads to this place. Our faith becomes manipulative. Our senses are eventually dulled. Our vocation is sold into slavery. The great exploration shrinks into petty self-obsessions. The competition crushes us. The hope of sex double-crosses. Where God is abandoned and self becomes center, the whole world begins to contract. It has all been a trap. We are betrayed. We betray ourselves.

So, Samson prayed. "O Lord GOD, please remember me and please strengthen me only this once, O God, that I may be avenged on the Philistines for my two eyes" (Judg. 16:28). Like before, Samson's eyes represent more than mere sight.

Now, blinded by his Philistine captors, Samson prayed to have his eyes avenged. Samson wanted to make right what had been lost—what he had seen wrongly so many times before. Samson realized that to be avenged would take divine intervention. On his own, there was little he could now accomplish.

The biblical concept of vengeance has more to do with our own dependence on God's salvation than it does revenge. Samson had finally realized that his life was dependent on the story of God's work, not his own strength or adventure.

I think Samson was praying that his lack of sight—both physically and spiritually—wouldn't be the thing for which he was remembered. He was praying for all of his failures to be made right. He was praying for vindication—to have another chance to live for a better story. Blinded, Samson could now see things more clearly than he ever had before.

TRUE ADVENTURE REQUIRES DISCERNMENT

This may be the most important thing you can learn about your instinct for adventure: what you think you need is often wrong. What you think matters is often the opposite. What you think a meaningful life should feel like is rarely what it does. Your heart and your eyes will betray you. Untrained, they are not to be trusted. Your search for adventure too often costs you your better commitments: relationships, marriage, children, careers, place, and even God. What you need are new eyes and a new heart. Eyes that can see the adventure God already has you on and a heart that can commit to it. As Marcel Proust put it, "The real voyage of discovery consists not in seeking new landscapes but in having new eyes."[6]

There is a risk of being lured away from your commitments by some call to a better adventure, but that risk is always secondary to the risk that your lack of discernment will keep you from recognizing the adventure God already has you in. To follow God, you must learn to taste well what He is giving you in this place. There is no better place to recognize God than in the place you are. As one poet explained to his student, "If your daily life seems poor, do not blame it; blame yourself, tell yourself that you are not poet enough to call forth its riches; for to the creator there is no poverty and no poor indifferent place."[7]

If the experiences of your day—the sights and sounds of your particular place—seem dull and meaningless, don't blame them; blame yourself. You haven't cultivated a taste for recognizing the complexity of God's presence in that place. You scrape out the honey and miss its message. You trade the divine for silly banter. You give up God's unique work to be like everyone else.

You'll never find the adventure you're looking for until you learn to commit to the one you're already in. When you do, the world will explode in senses of the Spirit's work. God's hand becomes apparent in every tucked-away corner of life. Your true adventure is here, recognizing the story God has placed you in. Your problem is not a lack of adventure; your problem is a lack of discernment for recognizing it.

One of the great adventure stories I know is Tolkien's *Lord of the Rings*. At the center of that story is a character who, much like you, has to abandon his conception of adventure for the reality of the one at hand. Near the end of his journey to destroy the ring, Frodo sensed fully the weight of his task. Tolkien calls it the "dark hour of weariness."[8] Overcome by the bleakness of his situation, Frodo cursed all that surrounded him: the stones, the earth, the air, the water. It wasn't the danger of armies or magic that now plagued him, it was the monotony, the endlessness of the task, and the sense of what felt like an impossible goal. The story no longer felt like the adventure he had imagined when it all began. Courage and optimism buoyed him at the beginning; now, it just felt hard and unending.

Frodo and his friend Sam sat for a moment in those shadows of Mordor and began to discuss how some adventures are chosen but how the real ones cannot be. The anxiety of their experience was what a true adventure felt like. As Sam suggested:

> "We shouldn't be here at all, if we'd known more about it before we started. But I suppose it's often that way. The brave things in the old tales and songs . . . adventures, as I used to call them. I used to think that they were things the wonderful folk of the stories went out and looked for, because they wanted them, because they were exciting and life was a bit dull. . . . But that's not the way of it with the tales that really mattered, or the ones that stay in the mind. Folk seem to have been just landed in them, usually—their paths were laid that way, as you put it. But I expect they had lots of chances, like us, of turning back, only they didn't. And if they had, we shouldn't know, because they'd have been forgotten. . . . I wonder what sort of a tale we've fallen into?"
>
> "I wonder," said Frodo. "But I don't know. And that's the way of a real tale."[9]

I wonder about that same question for your life. What kind of tale have you fallen into? What story is God working? What adventure is unfolding just beneath your recognition of it?

Maybe the meaninglessness and boredom are exactly what real adventures are meant to feel like. The trying scenes of life are a terrible place to draw final conclusions about who you are or what the author is doing—you simply haven't reached the end to know. The best stories never feel grand in the moments along the way. In a true adventure, the uncertainty must be accepted from the beginning, with almost nothing else known. The danger and physical trials are not what makes the story; they are only the setting for what really counts—great adventures advance on faith. The real tension is always the internal battle for belief—faith to stay the course. Faith to believe a story exists where others have given up on it. Faith to believe something is happening even when it doesn't feel like it. Adventure is always a story of that commitment.

> **Adventure is not a sin, but when it lacks discernment and costs commitment it inevitably leads to betrayal and ruin.**

Adventure is not a sin, but when it lacks discernment and costs commitment it inevitably leads to betrayal and ruin. Have your adventure, but never at the cost of commitment. And commit yourself to a kind of discernment that doesn't need distant shores or adrenaline-fueled feats to feel it. Learn to recognize and taste fully the adventure already at hand.

HIS HAIR BEGAN TO GROW

Sitting in that dark prison cell, we read a simple turn in Samson's story: "But the hair of his head began to grow again" (Judg. 16:22). That is the stroke of literary genius: poetic, understated, and life-changing. The hair that had been shaved grew back.

There is nothing miraculous about hair growth. Your hair is growing right now, but for Samson, that realization came with life-affirming hope. All was not lost. How had the Philistines not remembered to cut it? But Samson's story could not be shaved away. His discarded calling was dormant ground waiting for that sprout of new life to break through the disappointments.

Samson hadn't done it. He hadn't forced the strands of hair out of their follicles. As G. K. Chesterton put it, "You cannot grow a beard in a moment of passion."[10] With his hands shackled to the wall behind him, he may not have even known that it was forming on his scalp. Forces were at work which he didn't need to control or even recognize. His strength was returning—his adventure reforming—not because of his effort, but in spite of it. As David Jackman wrote in his commentary on Judges, Samson's story "begins with a strong man who is revealed to be weak, but it ends with a weak man who is stronger than ever he was before."[11]

Without this moment, Samson's story is nothing more than a life wasted. But this fresh growth of hair suggests something quite different. The most important characteristics of who you are and where your life is going aren't in your control. Close your eyes, bear down, and see if you can get your hair to grow. You can't. It is yours—your hair—but you are dependent on some force at work which you can't direct. Things are developing in you which you have no control over. It cost Samson everything to finally discern it.

In the end, he tasted of the riches of God's grace, a taste which can only be cultivated by faith, by embracing God's bigger story through a deepening commitment to the adventure He has you on.

Your better adventure is before you; you need only the courage to abandon your own and the faith to receive the one God is leading. Receive it. Commit yourself more deeply to it. I wonder what kind of tale you have fallen into? Your real adventure is developing the discernment—new eyes—to find out.

* * *

Recognize your instinct for adventure.
Recognize your need for discernment and commitment.

Chapter 5

AMBITION:
A PROMISED LAND LOST

THE MOSES STORY: EXODUS–DEUTERONOMY

"At the age of six I wanted to be a cook. At seven I wanted
to be Napoleon. And my ambition has been growing steadily
ever since."

SALVADOR DALI

"Sabbath ceasing means to cease not only from work itself,
but also from the need to accomplish and be productive, from
the worry and tension that accompany our modern criterion
of efficiency, from our efforts to be in control of our lives as if
we were God, from our possessiveness and our enculturation,
and, finally, from the humdrum and meaninglessness that result
when life is pursued without the Lord at the center of it all."

MARVA J. DAWN

Martin Luther King Jr. began his speech from the steps of
the Lincoln Memorial by declaring that their gathering that day
would "go down in history as the greatest demonstration for
freedom in the history of our nation."[1] King was prophetic in so
many ways. His words on that August day of 1963 have become
one of the most remembered speeches of world history and, as he
predicted, a symbol of freedom that will not be soon forgotten.

With the strength and cadence of an Old Testament prophet, King declared to the crowd of more than 250,000 demonstrators, "I have a dream that my four little children will one day live in a nation where they will not be judged by the color of their skin but by the content of their character. I have a dream today!"

King's words were visionary. He painted a picture of a day to come, a possibility of who we could be as a nation. For many, that potential still seemed impossible, too far into the distance to be a reality, but King's clarity of speech and vision inspired generations to believe. There is a good reason that speech is so well remembered.

Far less known, but equally remarkable in its prophetic vision, was the final speech of King's life. Assassinated on the evening of April 4, 1968, King had delivered his final public address the night before at the Mason Temple in Memphis, Tennessee. So much had happened in the five years between those two speeches, but so much was still left to be done. King concluded his remarks that night with these words:

Well, I don't know what will happen now. We've got some difficult days ahead. But it doesn't matter with me now. Because I've been to the mountaintop. And I don't mind. Like anybody, I would like to live a long life. Longevity has its place. But I'm not concerned about that now. I just want to do God's will. And He's allowed me to go up to the mountain. And I've looked over. And I've seen the promised land. I may not get there with you. But I want you to know tonight, that we, as a people, will get to the promised land. And I'm happy, tonight. I'm not worried about anything. I'm not fearing any man. Mine eyes have seen the glory of the coming of the Lord.[2]

He had no way of knowing that the next day would be his last. His life would not be a witness to longevity, but a witness to his enduring vision. The possibility that he would not live to see it a reality would prove true. In only a few hours, King would be cut down by an assassin's bullet.

I'm so moved by his perspective on that final night of his life, his ability to believe so deeply in a cause but to not need to be at the center of it or to have it fulfilled before his eyes. King had hold of something so much greater than himself. His ambition for that better day didn't rob him of his contentment and joy for being faithful in the moment. He found his companion in that greatest of biblical prophets, Moses. King, in his final recorded paragraph, turned his attention to the death of Moses who stood on Mount Nebo looking toward his own promised land, which he too realized he would not know, would not feel beneath his feet, in this life. They both bore witness to a higher instinct than ambition.

A DREAM SO CLOSE

From the mountaintop, Moses could see far into the distance. From Gilead to Dan, the land of Naphtali, Ephraim, Manasseh, and all the way to the Mediterranean. He could see the desert of the Negev and the palms of Jericho, the whole of that long-awaited promised land unfolded before him.

It's hard to imagine just what that view must have meant to Moses. Even today, the view is breathtaking in its scale and historical significance, but for Moses, those rocky ridges and shaded valleys, the Mediterranean haze, and the meandering Jordan valley meant so much more than scenery.

I see Moses, weary and short of breath from his climb, finding a place against a rock, now leaned back against it with his face turned to the west. Behind him, as the sun broke over the peak of Nebo, it spilled light down onto the land, the colors shifting as each geographic feature emerged from the long shadows. There it all was, finally. His promised land.

It was the fulfillment of forty years spent leading Israel through the wilderness and forty more of shepherding in obscurity, and still another forty learning and growing in his adopted Egyptian home. That land was the culmination of his life's work, crossing into it, the definitive finish line of success, the realization of his highest ambition.

What did he feel? Joy? Relief? Exhaustion? How could he not be overwhelmed by it and by God's faithfulness to a promise which had always seemed so far away?

Now, he was this close; could see it, smell it, hear it. Then the Lord spoke to Moses on that mountain. "This is the land of which I swore to Abraham, to Isaac, and to Jacob, 'I will give it to your offspring.' I have let you see it with your eyes, but you shall not go over there" (Deut. 34:4). Moses would be allowed to see the promised land but never to step foot into it.

How hard it must have been to hear those words, but somewhere deep within, he knew it would be this way. Like those he had led, he too had faltered, had failed to trust and fully believe. That final goal of his work would be left, for him, unfinished. Moses didn't protest.

Seated there on that mountain, Deuteronomy records simply, "So Moses the servant of the Lord died there in the land of Moab, according to the word of the Lord" (Deut. 34:5). As Aaron Wildavsky put it, "Moses fades into his book. His story gives way to Joshua's and Israel's. He had taken Israel to that land, but he would not enter it."[3]

It is too easy to read Moses's story as a holy man forced to constantly deal with the complaining and grumbling Israelites. Moses, the resolute leader, pressing on through sea and desert. Where their convictions falter, he pulled them through. Moses is the image of conviction, determination, and drive. Destined for something great, Moses carried his people to their freedom. When they could only remember how to be slaves, it was his vision and ambition that formed them into a new nation.

But that's only partly true. Pay closer attention, and a much fuller and more human image of Israel's leader emerges. Moses was a man of ambition and he was a man who knew the disillusionment of failure. He was like so many of us who struggle to keep our ambitions in their proper place.

Moses's death on Mount Nebo seems unfair. It's not the way we want his story to end—or ours. But Moses didn't see it that way. He died, as he had been at his best, with hope and contentment. This prohibition was God's way of forcing Moses to recognize things about himself which leadership, success, and ambition tend to obscure from men. It is our lesson to learn too. How easily our ambitions replace our God. How easily the finish line replaces the process.

THE DISILLUSIONMENT OF AMBITION

Ambition is one of those topics which I find, though constantly experienced, is rarely discussed. It's too complicated and too difficult to discern which parts of our ambitions are holy and which are just desperation or plain old vanity. We all know that ambition has driven men to achieve great things and has driven many, and sometimes the same men, into destructive self-obsession and narcissistic abuses. Ambition is like that syringe of life-saving medicine. It takes a wise doctor to understand its proper dose. Too much may kill just as quickly as too little, but just enough can preserve a life.

From a young age, we are encouraged in our ambitions. You can be anything you want to be. Dream big. Reach for the stars. Who says to their six-year-old son, "You really don't have any chance of playing in the big leagues or being president; you might as well settle for something more realistic"? No, we encourage the dreaming, the possibility, the ambition, and the drive.

Moses, rescued and raised by an Egyptian princess, would have had every possibility before him. Being prince of Egypt meant no personal ambition was out of reach. In the book of Acts, Stephen reminded his audience that "Moses was instructed in all the wisdom of the Egyptians, and he was mighty in his words and deeds" (Acts 7:22). At the time of his birth, no civilization possessed the knowledge and possibility of Egypt. As a part of the royal family, Moses would have been trained to build and govern kingdoms. Personal tutors—the best in all of the world—would have taught him about culture, religion, politics, medicine, law, mathematics, architecture, and war. Moses would have been trained physically, disciplining himself in fitness, horsemanship, archery, and hand-to-hand combat. His was the greatest education available to anyone on earth. There was no limit to the potential he could achieve.

Though every possible luxury lay before him, Moses found himself intrigued by the plight of the Hebrew slaves. Egypt was a world power, accumulating and assimilating skilled people wherever they found them, but somehow Moses came to identify with his humble roots. The book of Exodus tells us that, "One day, when Moses had grown up, he went out to his people and looked on their burdens" (Ex. 2:11).

You can imagine him behind some glistening chariot of white horses, clothed in his royal robe, a gold hilted sword strapped to his side, the cultic symbols of Egypt's gods adorned in his jewelry; he sat on that hill looking down on the lines of tattered Hebrew slaves stomping out mud bricks, bundles of them loaded on their shoulders. Beneath the robes and riches, he was one of them. His blood was the same as theirs. He knew it. He felt something new he hadn't before, a new ambition.

Just then, he saw an Egyptian master beating one of these Hebrew men—one of his own. Looking around and finding no one else near, Moses struck the Egyptian and killed him. He quickly buried the Egyptian's body in the sand.

Was this a moment of overpowering passion? Had it been premeditated? Was it a momentary guilt for his privileged position, his participation in the power system which oppressed his people, or was it a deliberate effort to kick off a rebellion, to take a position as the leader who would deliver them? The New Testament suggests that Moses "supposed that his brothers would understand that God was giving them salvation by his hand" (Acts 7:25). It was an ambition that motivated Moses to act—salvation by his hand.

There is an extrabiblical story in the Jewish Midrashic commentaries that attempts to fill in this question of Moses's character and intent.[4] The story goes that as a toddler, Moses would often sit and play in Pharaoh's lap. Seeing the glistening jewels of his crown, Moses reached up and took it off Pharaoh's head and placed it on his own. Superstitious, Pharaoh feared that it was an omen. Calling his advisors, Pharaoh demanded to know if it was a sign of things to come. He was prepared to put the child to death if the child's actions revealed a coming threat to his own power.

The advisors decided to put the toddler to a test. They set two bowls before Moses, one filled with gold and the other with glowing embers. If he reached for the gold, they would conclude his motives were for Pharaoh's position. As they watched, Moses began to reach for the gold, but the hand of an angel stopped him and redirected him to the embers. Taking a piece of the fire, Moses touched it to his lips, burning his tongue but saving his life. The story also offers an explanation for why Moses would later claim to be slow of speech.

The Bible makes no reference to this story, but it demonstrates how many ancient Jews thought about Moses and those early years in Egypt. Moses was characterized as a person of ambitious reach. As Shakespeare put it, "Who doth ambition shun?"[5] We all feel it. But we all struggle with what to make of it, what to do with it.

Was it this ambition that moved Moses to murder? Was it that deep-seated ever-present ambition—a child reaching for a crown—that now swelled in Moses as he reached again and struck down the Egyptian slave master? Was Moses now reaching for another kind of crown?

The next day, seeing two fellow Hebrews fighting, Moses again intervened. But they would have none of it. "Who made you a prince and a judge over us? Do you mean to kill me as you killed the Egyptian?" (Ex. 2:14).

Moses's secret was out, but their rejection of his effort was a much deeper blow. There would be penalties for murdering an Egyptian; not even his royal position could save him from that.

But I think Moses felt more than the fear of repercussion. Moses had taken his first step toward his life's greatest ambition and not only had he failed, but he was mocked by those he sought to save. The spark that had ignited his vision was quickly snuffed by their taunting rejection. Humiliated and exposed, Moses fled into obscurity.

THE PERPLEXING EXPERIENCE OF AMBITION

The next period of Moses's life was marked by his own wilderness. He made his living as a shepherd working for his father-in-law. Forty years passed with nothing apparently worth recording, nothing but days in the field with sheep, family meals, and raising kids. It would be forty years of this obscurity before Moses encountered the burning bush. How his days in Egypt must have seemed like a lifetime ago. How the Hebrews' cause must have faded in his mind. What had become of Moses's ambition? Had the wilderness withered it away? Does time loosen ambition's grip?

Then, unexpectedly, the burning bush. God spoke to Moses. "Then the Lord said, 'I have surely seen the affliction of my people who are in Egypt and have heard their cry because of their taskmasters. I know their sufferings, and I have come down to deliver them out of the hand of the Egyptians. . . . Come, I will send you to Pharaoh that you may bring my people, the children of Israel, out of Egypt'" (Ex. 3:7–10).

Was this not exactly what Moses had envisioned forty years earlier? Had he not already tried? Had this not been the very ambition for which he had sacrificed his place of power and opulence, identifying with the suffering of his people? What must it have meant to now hear the divine voice calling him back to the task he had assumed long lost? But it would take more than fire in a bush to convince Moses to take the risk again.

After many questions and doubts, Moses finally admitted his reluctance to obey. "Lord, please send someone else" (Ex. 4:13). Where was the ambition? Where was the possibility? How can the New Testament describe Moses as profound in speech when Moses thought of himself as slow? How could Moses act so decisively before and now struggle to even entertain the possibility of acting at all? How can this be the same Moses?

Anyone who has honestly wrestled with purpose and their own failures understands that these two dispositions of Moses are not a conflict but the lived experience of our ambitions. Ambition has a way of leading us into two extremes. At times ambition can be so burning hot that it consumes all of us, filling us with a sense of limitless potential. But that same ambition can just as quickly become our accuser and mock us into disbelief. The experience of ambition's confidence and ambition's disillusionment is far more connected than we often admit. And between these two extremes lies the more common experience of confusion. Ambition makes everything seem possible, yet always just out of reach. It's exhausting and demoralizing.

John Calvin understood the perplexing nature of ambition. He explained, "Those who yield themselves up to the influence of ambition will soon lose themselves in a labyrinth of perplexity."[6] Or consider Victor Hugo's warning in *Les Misérables*, "Who knows how easily ambition disguises itself under the name of a calling, possibly in good faith, and deceiving itself, in sanctimonious confusion."[7] Hugo and Calvin echo what is a common suspicion across history's many writers and philosophers. Ambition aids men in many good pursuits, but to handle it well, one must become its master and acquire the skills necessary to recognize its destructive tendencies or risk being lost in its maze of twisting emotions and desires. Ambition is confusing.

Maybe the greatest risk of ambition is its tendency to confuse our place with God's. This is the most dangerous kind of confusion. The philosopher Kierkegaard explained, "The proud person always wants to do the right thing, the great thing. But because he wants to do it in his own strength, he is fighting not with man but with God."[8]

GOD HATES VISIONARY DREAMING

Somewhere in the earliest years of my pastoral vocation, I came across a thin book titled simply *Life Together*. It was written in the late 1930s by a German named Dietrich Bonhoeffer. Bonhoeffer was a theologian and professor living in Nazi-controlled Germany. He was one of the great theological minds of his age and, though young, was quickly making a name for himself internationally. Gifted with so much potential, the great challenge of his life would be the rise of Nazism in his home country and his place in that uncertain moment of history.

In 1930, Bonhoeffer was able to travel to the US to participate in a teaching fellowship at Union Seminary in New York City. Many were beginning to anticipate the coming conflict in Europe, and Bonhoeffer was encouraged to stay in the safety of the United States. But Bonhoeffer felt a deep conviction to return. He was strongly opposed to Hitler's vision for Germany. Hitler had already begun pressuring German churches into compliance and allegiance to his socialist party. Bonhoeffer would be a voice of opposition to Hitler's efforts, and he hoped to be a part of rebuilding

Germany after Hitler's defeat, which he considered inevitable.

Upon returning, Bonhoeffer led an underground seminary, training pastors for work in those dangerous and hostile conditions. Bonhoeffer was eventually discovered and arrested for his role in a plot to assassinate Hitler. On April 9, 1945, just two weeks before his prison was liberated by US troops and just three weeks before Berlin fell to the Soviets, Bonhoeffer was led naked into the prison's courtyard and hanged. He had been executed on orders given by Hitler himself. Bonhoeffer died, never seeing Hitler's final defeat.

I wonder, like Moses staring at that promised land he would never enter, had it all been enough for Bonhoeffer? Could he not have imagined more? He had so much more to do. What if he had stayed in the US? What if his execution had been delayed just a few more days? Had he not imagined more of his life beyond that day, beyond those Nazi gallows?

A doctor present in the prison was said to have later recounted his observations of Bonhoeffer's death. "The prisoners . . . were taken from their cells, and the verdicts of the court martial read out to them. Through the half-open door in one room of the huts, I saw Pastor Bonhoeffer, before taking off his prison garb, kneeling on the floor praying fervently to his God. I was most deeply moved by the way this lovable man prayed, so devout and so certain that God heard his prayer. At the place of execution, he again said a prayer and then climbed the steps to the gallows, brave and composed. His death ensued in a few seconds. In the almost fifty years that I have worked as a doctor, I have hardly ever seen a man die so entirely submissive to the will of God."[9]

While reading Bonhoeffer's *Life Together,* I came across the sentence, "God hates visionary dreaming."[10] The simplicity of that statement caught me off guard, not to mention it challenged everything I had ever learned about church leadership and vision.

Bonhoeffer continued, "It makes the dreamer proud and pretentious. The man who fashions a visionary ideal of community demands that it be realized by God, by others, and by himself. He enters the community of Christians with his demands, sets up his own law, and judges the brethren and God himself

> Too often, our ambitions for a better life cost us the one we already possess.

accordingly. . . . When things do not go his way, he calls the effort a failure. When his ideal picture is destroyed, he sees the community going to smash. So he becomes, first the accuser of his brethren, then an accuser of God and finally the despairing accuser of himself."

I'm not sure I have ever read anything which convicted me as deeply as those words. Too often, our ambitions for a better life cost us the one we already possess. Bonhoeffer would add, "The sin of irritability that blossoms so quickly in the community shows again and again how much inordinate ambition, and thus how much unbelief, still exists."[11] Ambition so easily leads to unbelief. Our ambitions and our attempts to measure our progress rob us of trust in God.

Our vision becomes the standard by which we judge ourselves, others, and God. We become God's judge, measuring Him against the fulfillment of our own expectations. When we fail, we look for someone to blame: the people who hold us back or get in our way, our own lack of discipline or talent, and even our Creator—the one who has failed to create us adequately or answer our most ambitious prayers. Finally, we become our own accuser and slide into self-loathing and discouragement. An ambition which we cannot forfeit is always a sign of unbelief. We look suspiciously toward God and man. We expose our inability to trust Him.

The English poet Alexander Pope called ambition "the glorious fault of angels and of gods."[12] And Shakespeare likewise recommended, "I charge thee, fling away ambition. By that sin fell the angels; how can man then, the image of his Maker, hope to win by it?"[13]

Eugene Peterson wisely warned, "Our culture encourages and rewards ambition without qualification. We are surrounded by a way of life in which betterment is understood as expansion, as acquisition, as fame. . . . There is nothing recent about the temptation. It is the oldest sin in the book, the one that got Adam thrown out of the garden and Lucifer tossed out of heaven. What is fairly new about it is the general admiration and approval that it receives."[14]

AMBITION AS DISBELIEF

Moses did eventually comply with God's call to lead Israel out of Egypt, but his task was a constant temptation to mistake his own work for God's, his evaluation of success against God's calling to faithfulness. At the center of Moses's story is the temptation to allow his ambition to mistake his place for God's. If you find handling your ambition perplexing, don't worry; Moses also struggled to sort it out. Let me show you.

Israel was a reluctant and complaining people. They complained of not having water and of not having food and then of not having the right kind of food. They blamed God, but mostly they questioned Moses. Moses's own family undermined his leadership, and there were rebellions that had to be put down. While Moses stood on the mountain receiving God's law for the people, below they were ready to abandon him and cast their own golden image of God.

God was furious and determined to destroy Israel and begin again. But Moses interceded. He did so in an intriguing way. "Moses said to the people, 'You have sinned a great sin. And now I will go up to the LORD; perhaps I can make atonement for your sin'" (Ex. 32:30). It was an audacious idea—one man atoning for the sins of a rebellious nation. But Moses went back to the Lord and said, "Now, if you will forgive their sin—but if not, please blot me out of your book that you have written" (Ex. 32:31–32).

It's a remarkable statement. Moses offers his life as an atonement for the people's sins. Who wouldn't marvel at his commitment, his resolve? But God seemed almost indifferent to Moses's offer. God responded simply, "Whoever has sinned against me, I will blot out of my book. But now go, lead the people to the place about which I have spoken to you" (Ex. 32:33–34).

As we continue reading Moses's story, a similar event took place in the book of Numbers. Again, the people were complaining and ready to abandon Moses and God's plan. God had been feeding them miraculously with manna from heaven, but the people cried out for meat. "We remember the fish we ate in Egypt that cost nothing, the cucumbers, the melons, the leeks, the onions, and the garlic. But now our strength is dried up, and there is nothing at all but this manna to look at" (Num. 11:5–6).

Again, the Lord was angry. Again, Moses went before Him. And again, Moses's death was the topic of conversation, but this time Moses's motives were made explicitly clear.

Moses complained too. "Why have you dealt ill with your

servant? And why have I not found favor in your sight, that you lay the burden of all this people on me? . . . I am not able to carry all this people alone; the burden is too heavy for me. If you will treat me like this, kill me at once, if I find favor in your sight, that I may not see my wretchedness'" (Num. 11:11–15).

Again, Moses offers his life, but this time not as a sacrifice. He offers his life to be done with these people. "Kill me so I can be done with it all." "Kill me before I'm ruined." Again, God gave little attention to Moses's words. He sent Moses back to his work and gave the Israelites quail to eat.

Still, the people continued to complain. Next it was a lack of water. God heard them and instructed Moses to speak to the rock, which would produce water for the people. God would once more deliver them through miraculous provision. But this time, Moses had had enough. He gathered Israel before the rock, and he began to chastise them. "'Hear now, you rebels: shall we bring water for you out of this rock?' And Moses lifted up his hand and struck the rock with his staff twice, and water came out abundantly, and the congregation drank" (Num. 20:10–11).

It's hard not to feel for Moses, stuck with these constantly complaining people, but Moses's motives become clearer as the story unfolds. Where once he would have died for them, now his disdain is palpable. Where before he petitioned God on their behalf, now he speaks as if he is God's equal. "Shall *we* bring water for you?"

Moses's ambitions had led him to places of great achievement and to places of sorrow and self-pity, but finally it led him to disobedience and pride, which mistook his own anger and frustration for God's. He had once been reluctant to speak for God; now he instinctively fills in what he would have God say. It might seem small, striking the rock when God had commanded him to speak to it, but having tracked this growing resentment, it's not hard to see Moses's actions for what they were. It was an outburst of frustration and disappointment. They had not been the people he expected them to be. It had not gone as he imagined it would go. He had lost his ability to separate himself from God, his work from God's work, and his ambition from his actual calling. As our ambitions are prone to do, Moses lost his ability to distinguish his own emotions from God's.

Again, Eugene Peterson helps us understand:

> It is additionally difficult to recognize unruly ambition as a sin because it has a kind of superficial relationship to the virtue of aspiration—an impatience with mediocrity and a dissatisfaction with all things created until we are at home with the Creator, the hopeful striving for the best God has for us. . . . But if we take the energies that make for aspiration and remove God from the picture, replacing him with our own crudely sketched self-portrait, we end up with ugly arrogance. . . . Ambition is aspiration gone crazy. . . . Ambition takes these same energies for growth and development and uses them to make something tawdry and cheap, sweatily knocking together a Babel when we could be vacationing in Eden.[15]

If ambition risks mistaking what we would have God do for what He is actually doing, then surely Moses's burst of anger is a sign of this dark and unchecked ambition at work. Where before God had mostly ignored Moses's self-indulgence, here God spoke directly to it. "Because you did not believe in me, to uphold me as holy in the eyes of the people of Israel, therefore you shall not

THE 5 MASCULINE INSTINCTS

bring this assembly into the land that I have given them" (Num. 20:12). Moses had not trusted God to be God. His ambitions got in the way.

Is it possible that the desperation of your own ambitions keeps you from trusting and honoring Him too? Is it possible that your ambitions have shifted your relationship with God into one of expectation and demand? You live to constantly judge how God and everyone else is living up to your expectations. Unfulfilled, your ambitions leave you vulnerable to the same bitterness and charges of unfairness. Your ambitions risk mistaking what God is doing for what you would have Him do. It is possible that your ambitions are leading you ever closer to that same disobedience and unbelief.

A CHECK ON AMBITION

God has long offered a way of checking the instinct of our ambitions. In fact, Moses had once understood this better dependence on God.

Early in leading Israel, Moses had sought help from God, an explanation of how He would do it. How would He lead that reluctant nation of Israel to the promised land?

> To be human, a mature one at least, is to recognize our limits.

God's response is interesting. The Lord replied to Moses, "My presence will go with you, and I will give you rest" (Ex. 33:14). A leading presence makes sense, but Moses hadn't asked about rest. Ambition stirs us to action; who is thinking about rest? What does rest have to do with reaching the promised land? They could rest when they arrived.

I think what Moses finally found, sitting on Mount Nebo and looking at the land he knew he would never lead Israel into, was that rest. His work had ended. It had not been finished. Moses had not completed what he had long set out to do. But he was made to put it down. To lay down the burden and to sit before his unfulfilled promise.

The great Jewish novelist Kafka wrote of Moses, "He is on the track of Canaan all his life; it is incredible that he should see the land only when on the verge of death. The dying vision of it can only be intended to illustrate how incomplete a moment is human life. . . . Moses fails to enter Canaan not because his life is too short but because it is a human life."[16]

Moses is reminded of his humanity. To be human, a mature one at least, is to recognize our limits. Do we ever achieve all that we imagined we would? Is life not always a coming to terms with what is left undone? There are works that we do not complete. There are callings which never arrive. There are promises we take with us into that next life. And we, along with Moses, are trained to embrace that uncertainty, not by the burdens we can carry, but by the burdens we can lay down. We are trained to see it not in our moments of doing but in our moments of rest.

God's people have long learned to check their ambition through the self-imposed practice of rest, what the Bible calls sabbath.

It is a shame that in our day sabbath is so rarely understood or practiced. I too frequently hear it taught as a tool of optimization. We rest so that we can be more efficient on the other six days. We take one day slow, so we have the energy to take the other six faster. A sabbath practiced in an attempt to life-hack more productivity out of the other six is to miss the point entirely. Sabbath is never a strategy to get more done.

We would do well to take Leo Tolstoy's advice offered to the men of his own day. He wrote, "If, then, I were asked for the most important advice I could give, that which I considered to be the most useful to the men of our century, I should simply say: in the name of God, stop a moment, cease your work, look around you."[17] That's the best definition of sabbath I know. In the name of God, just stop for a moment. Put down what you're working on. Look around you. What have you been missing?

You need an intentional check on what you can accomplish. I know, in this world that sounds crazy. But that is a sabbath. That was what God gave Moses. You need to do less, not more. For without a sabbath, you'll be hard-pressed to recognize God. You'll be busy trying to justify your existence and rushing right past what God is doing. Worse, you risk imagining you're doing things for Him, just as He is asking you to stop and receive from Him.

So, just stop. Check yourself. Stop being so desperate for that promotion. Stop with the goal setting. Stop with the to-do lists. Stop trying to make things happen. Stop trying to be someone. Stop worrying about your career. Stop worrying about how you're going to make a living. Stop dreaming and wishing. For just one day a week, in the name of God, stop.

Then look around. The world didn't fall over while you were stopped. There is more to what God is doing than what you have been doing. Sabbath is a tool for perspective, for intentionally checking the hustle of your ambition. It helps you see things about yourself that your ambition has a tendency to obscure. It helps you see things about God and others too.

Stopping is hard work at first but so much depends on it.

You must intentionally do less than you are capable of doing. You must achieve less than you could possibly achieve. You must force margins at the cost of efficiency. You must strive for less than your ambition can imagine. Teach yourself to be suspicious of what you can't let go of. Teach yourself to suspect that which is most difficult for you to lay down.

As C. S. Lewis warned a friend, "Don't be too easily convinced that God really wants you to do all sorts of work you needn't do. . . . There can be intemperance in work just as in drink. What feels like zeal may be only fidgets or even the flattering of one's self-importance."[18] Sabbath and rest is always the test of inordinate ambition.

NOT EVEN FOR A GOLD MEDAL

One of the best lessons of sabbath I know comes from the life of Eric Liddell. You've probably seen the movie *Chariots of Fire*, but the movie leaves out some of the most important details of Liddell's life.

Liddell was one of the 1920s most accomplished runners. In 1924, he was training for the hundred-meter race in the Paris Olympics. He was favored to win the gold, that is, until the race schedule was posted, and Liddell realized the opening rounds were scheduled for July 6th, a Sunday.

Liddell was a devout Christian. For years he had refused to compete on Sundays. It was his conviction for keeping the sabbath holy. Much to the frustration of his coaches and fans, he stood by his convictions. He simply refused to run on a Sunday, even at the Olympics. He would not compete in the Olympic hundred-meter race he had qualified for and was favored to win.

Since childhood, Liddell had struggled with two ambitions: his love for running and a call to missionary work. He had wanted to become a missionary to China, but he was also fast, and he loved to run. There is a famous line in the movie: "I believe God made me for a purpose, but he also made me fast! And when I run I feel His pleasure."[19] That line is famous, but it serves in the movie to draw a contrast with his chief competitor, Harold Abrahams. Equally fast, Abrahams explained his obsession with running differently. "I will raise my eyes and look down that corridor, four-feet wide, with only ten seconds to justify my whole existence."[20]

Abrahams had all of the clarity and focus we know it takes to be the best at something, and he was willing to make the sacrifices to do it. His ambition controlled everything. Eric Liddell's life had none of that simplicity. He seemed torn in two directions. Though people now admire his conviction, at the time, it drove coaches and teammates nuts. I'm sure people told him to get serious about one or the other. "Run or be a missionary. Just don't do both halfway. You're wasting your talent." He came off looking like a self-righteous stick-in-the-mud, confused about who he wanted to be and on some crusade to prove a point.

Liddell didn't compete in the hundred-meter race at the Paris Olympics. He simply refused to run on the sabbath. Instead, he competed in the four-hundred-meter race, which was scheduled for a weekday. It was a race he had little experience with, but he not only won the gold, he also set a world record. Fans described his record-breaking run as inspired. It's a remarkable story, but I don't think the most important part was his medal.

In *The Flying Scotsman*, Sally Magnusson's biography of Liddell, she tells a little-known story that took place years later during Liddell's missions work in China. It was 1943, and Japan was marching across the Asian continent. Liddell had been captured and forced into a Japanese internment camp. A group of young boys and girls in the camp asked him to organize and referee a hockey game. Of course, it was a Sunday, and, as expected, Liddell refused. He gave them the gear and offered to join them another day. The next Sunday, the kids explained how their game had turned into a full-fledged fistfight, with some still showing the marks to prove it. So, what did Liddell do? He went out and joined them—on a Sunday. He would forfeit the Olympics but broke his sabbath to participate in a prison camp kids' game.

Magnusson writes, "He would not run on a Sunday for an Olympic gold medal in the 100 meters and all the glory in the world; but he refereed a game on Sunday, he broke his unbreakable principle, just to keep a handful of imprisoned youngsters at peace with each other."[21] Liddell's sabbath wasn't legalism. It wasn't about proving some saintly level of commitment. It wasn't about some legal, religious requirement. His sabbath was about intentionally limiting himself. Liddell used his sabbath to keep his running in its proper vocational place. He used it to check his ambition. He was more than a runner; his life was more than a single race. His identity was made for bigger categories. He knew he needed the sabbath to restrain his own ambition—not to be less, but to be more.

Where his colleagues saw confusion and a lack of focus, Liddell had peace and deep contentment. He ran because it pleased God. He kept the sabbath because there was nothing he needed to prove by running or winning. He was willing to sacrifice even an Olympic medal. For Liddell, a medal didn't mean that much. His ambition was for better things.

MAKE THIS YOUR AMBITION

Maybe one of the most neglected commands of Scripture is Paul's words to the Thessalonians. "Make it your ambition to lead a quiet life: You should mind your own business and work with your hands, just as we told you, so that your daily life may win the respect of outsiders" (1 Thess. 4:11–12 NIV). Christianity is not meant to keep you from achieving great things. Its goal is not to force you down and rob you of your potential, far from it. It is offering you a better ambition, an ambition that frees you from the desperation of proving yourself and earning your value. An ambition which keeps you from eclipsing and missing God.

> Freed from the desperate forms of self-ambition, you are capable of achieving things that obsession, anxiety, and desperation never can.

To do truly great things, you have to become a person content with achieving only small things. I think Moses's greatest moment was not what he achieved but what he was able to let go of. For letting go of his vision allowed him to rest in God and to help us learn to do the same.

Freed from the desperate forms of self-ambition, you are capable of achieving things that obsession, anxiety, and desperation never can. You are able to do all things. As Paul would also explain to the Philippians, "I know how to be brought low, and I know how to abound. In any and every circumstance, I have learned the secret of facing plenty and hunger, abundance and need. I can do all things through him who strengthens me"

(Phil. 4:12–13). Your greatest potential is in your contentment, your ability to trust and receive from Christ.

* * *

A few years ago, I heard a professor lecture on the story of Jesus' transfiguration. He was explaining the possible locations for the event and the likelihood that the mountain on which Jesus was transfigured was Mount Tabor, not far from the Sea of Galilee. As the disciples witnessed Jesus' transformation—as His appearance began to shine and His clothes became radiant with white light—the disciples also recognized that He was suddenly joined by Elijah and Moses.

Thinking of that scene, it suddenly struck me. Moses was in the promised land. He was standing there in the middle of the Galilean countryside with Jesus. He had made it. Not back in that worn-out body of his wilderness wandering, but here beside Christ transfigured—transformed.

Maybe the theological significance is minor, but I can't help being moved by that image. Nothing is lost. Nothing is wasted. Moses's acceptance of that forced rest hadn't cost him anything. It had allowed him to receive something far better. Checking your ambition doesn't cost you anything either; it allows you to see and receive things you could never have achieved by your own efforts.

Bonhoeffer put it this way, "We must be ready to allow ourselves to be interrupted by God. God will be constantly crossing our paths and canceling our plans. . . . It is a strange fact that Christians and even ministers frequently consider their work so important and urgent that they allow nothing to disturb them.

They think they are doing God a service in this, but actually they are disdaining God's 'crooked yet straight path.'"[22]

God's path is always crooked, at least by the measurement of our own ambitions. But there is no better path to that final promise than His. Check your ambition. Stop. Rest. The right path is not always the shortest or the straightest, but for those willing to go where He is leading, a promised land always awaits.

And isn't that final and satisfying sense of contentment—arrival—what all ambition is finally in search of?

* * *

Recognize your instinct for ambition.
Recognize your need for rest.

Chapter 6

REPUTATION: THE IMAGE OF A KING

THE DAVID STORY: 1 SAMUEL–2 SAMUEL

"The impostor is what he *does*. . .The impostor prompts us to attach importance to what has no importance, clothing with a false glitter what is least substantial and turning us away from what is real. The false self causes us to live in a world of delusion. The impostor is a liar. Our false self stubbornly blinds each of us to the light and the truth of our own emptiness and hollowness. We cannot acknowledge the darkness within."

BRENNAN MANNING

"A man who lies to himself, and believes his own lies, becomes unable to recognize truth, either in himself or in anyone else, and he ends up losing respect for himself and for others. When he has no respect for anyone, he can no longer love, and, in order to divert himself, having no love in him, he yields to his impulses, indulges in the lowest forms of pleasure, and behaves in the end like an animal. And it all comes from lying."

FYODOR DOSTOEVSKY

On the south side of the White House lawn stood the Jackson Magnolia, the oldest tree on the property. Planted in 1828, it has provided shade to thirty-eight presidents and their guests.

But the tree also had a secret; it was not what it appeared to be.

Named after its planter, President Andrew Jackson, the magnolia has earned a respected place in White House history for its tragic tale. The election of 1828 that ushered Jackson into the White House was as contentious as any modern election. Jackson's campaign had been barraged with accusations of his wife's marital infidelity and calls for resignation. Ultimately, Jackson prevailed, but the toll of the campaign on his personal life was evident to all.

Jackson's wife, Rachel, had been at the center of many of the political attacks. While in the midst of battling the accusations, tuberculosis took the life of the Jacksons' adopted son. Overcome by their son's death, Rachel sank deeper into depression. Just days before Jackson set out for his presidential inauguration, Rachel suffered a massive heart attack and died. For Jackson, it was the culmination of a remarkably difficult year, and he wasted no time in placing blame on his political enemies. At her funeral, Jackson expressed his sorrow with the words, "May God Almighty forgive her murderers as I know she forgave them! I never can!"[1]

Upon arriving—now a widower—to the White House, Jackson unpacked a fresh cutting from one of the magnolias on his and Rachel's Nashville home. Jackson had it planted just outside the south entrance as a memorial to his late wife.

It has been featured on White House cards, dinner china, and on a printing of the twenty-dollar bill. The tree is a part of American history and an anchor of the White House visage. So, you can imagine people's reactions when news began to break that the Jackson Magnolia was scheduled to be cut down by the Trump administration.

From the public's southern view of the tree, with its remarkable three-story height of tangled limbs, polished leaves, and thick pearl-like petals, it still appeared grand—the magnolia, a symbol of nobility and perseverance. The thought of its removal, of chainsaw teeth grinding its historical significance to sawdust, was unimaginable to historians and tourists alike. And, like so much in our time, the news went immediately viral with shocking accusations and outrageous headlines.

But in truth, the Jackson Magnolia was not what it appeared to be. The tree was a façade, barely a tree at all. If not for an elaborate system of hidden cables and structural supports neatly placed behind limbs and branches, the tree would have collapsed decades ago. The tree appeared as impressive as it ever had, but in reality, it was a thin veneer of bark held up by modern steel—a half-truth.

It was scheduled for removal because the inevitability of its disintegration posed too great a risk to those standing in its shade. Already the cabling had begun to pull through what was left of the wood. It was a matter of time until it collapsed.

A local arborist determined that the Jackson Magnolia was missing 75 percent of its structural integrity.[2] No matter the amount of propping up and tying down, no matter the efforts made to prune for appearance and disguise rot, the tree simply lacked the integrity to keep standing. It would assuredly collapse under the weight of its own limbs and blooms. Its appearance was not its truth. Its integrity had finally been compromised.

YOU ARE THE MAN

The prophet Nathan had done what for decades David had managed to evade. With just two words, the complexity of David's divided life, private and public, was finally collapsed into a single moment of truth: bare, raw, and inescapable. Nathan's revelation left no room for pretending, no room for hiding. The reputation of David collapsed with the truth of David.

For so long, he had lived two lives, the prestigious and lavish trappings of his royal palace secured by his heroic reputation for God's anointing, and, kept neatly in the shadows of that same palace, lapses of lust, murder, jealousy, prejudice, and desperation. David's historic achievements of defeating Goliath and securing a united Israelite throne had been matched only by his meticulously executed image campaigns and cover-ups. That a king should be found guilty of manipulating his public image is no great shock; grand things were at stake after all: a burgeoning nation and the aspiring icon of their anointed king. But the staggering depth of the gulf between David's public reputation and private truth was maintained at the cost of life, Uriah's, by divine judgment on David's own sons and, in so many painful ways, David himself. Deception always feeds off of true life, hollowing it out and starving it of its courage.

How could David not sense the coming collapse? How could David hold together two worlds so radically opposed to one another for so long? With the weight of gold resting on his head, not even the presence of a holy prophet could pierce the façade. Not until David found himself caught in the trap of Nathan's parable, with the catastrophic consequences of that prophetic finger pointed to him in humiliating exposure, was David forced to admit that his life was neither what it appeared to others nor what he had convinced himself of. No amount of power or control could ultimately gild over the hollowness of his soul. He was finally exposed.

How could it have come to the taking of Bathsheba to fulfill his sexual gratification? To a conspiracy to assassinate Uriah, her husband, and David's own friend? The naivety to believe he had gotten away with it. How easily he had put it out of his mind, to go on writing psalms and offering sacrifices, unpenetrated by it. This, a man after God's own heart? This, the heroic David?

But what might be most shocking about Nathan's confrontation is how obvious the whole setup had been. Nathan had found an audience with the king under the guise of an injustice that necessitated David's judicial opinion. The story went, a rich man with many sheep had visitors whom he was obligated to feed. Unwilling to dip into his own resources, he instead stole the single lamb of his poorest neighbor and butchered it for his banquet. The man had stolen what was not his and further impoverished an already poorer man.

Having just read of David's seizure of Bathsheba and his slaughter of Uriah, who couldn't recognize that David was this rich man? The parable isn't particularly clever, but rather rudimentary and glaringly obvious to the reader.

But something blinded David to the truth of his own life laid before him in that story. Something so obscured David's self-awareness that, without recognizing himself, he ordered his own execution. "As the LORD lives, the man who has done this deserves to die," David decreed (2 Sam. 12:5). To which, I imagine in a hushed tone, Nathan responded simply, "You're him." David didn't see it coming. He had lost sense of himself.

Parker Palmer, in his book *A Hidden Wholeness: The Journey Toward an Undivided Life*, explains how easily we lose the ability to recognize the truth of our own lives. He writes, "Here is the ultimate irony of the divided life: live behind a wall long enough, and the true self you tried to hide from the world disappears from your own view! The wall itself and the world outside it become all that you know. Eventually, you even forget that the wall is there—and that hidden behind it is someone called 'you.'"[3] David had become a hollowed shell of who he really was. He was lost in his own disguise. He was no longer able to recognize even himself.

It is unfortunate that David's story is often reduced to a man who hit a rough patch and made some bad decisions, but upon being confronted, demonstrated model repentance. As if being really good at repenting is somehow its own kind of cover-up for a life of perpetually bad decisions. We say to ourselves, "Look at how terrible he feels; he must deep down be a pretty good guy."

I think we are far too naive in our reading of David's story. Or maybe it is not naiveté but our own crude self-justifications, a whitewashing of David, which aids in whitewashing ourselves. But David's story is not the tale of a godly man with a momentary lapse of judgment. The real David is far too much like yourself for that kind of simplification. The real David story is a complicated and vulnerable struggle for truth—a battle waged between public reputation and personal integrity.

A few years ago, I preached through 1 and 2 Samuel, sharing the stories of Saul and David with my congregation. I was surprised by their reactions. There was a group that found the horrific and animalistic details of David's sins hard to stomach. How, they wondered, could a man convicted of what appears to be gross sexual misconduct and the callous murder of a friend be called a man after God's own heart? How can this be the great king of Israel, the father by which Jesus Christ Himself would be called the son of David?

But there was also another group, usually quieter in their response, who found me after service in the hallway or wrote to me in Sunday evening emails and admitted how much David's life resonated with their own. Their sins were not as horrific, but there was something about the bare honesty of David's struggles that touched each of them. Many men I know long to feel like a man whom God would befriend like David, whom God would call a man after His own heart, but they struggle to find that spiritual confidence, carrying so many of their own secrets.

THE ONE ASKED FOR

To understand the struggle of David's reputation, we need to first grasp the world of Saul. David was shaped by, and inherited, the landscape of Saul's kingship, but not before that royal image was first formed by the demand of the people. "There shall be a king over us, that we also may be like all the nations, and that our king may judge us and go out before us and fight our battles" (1 Sam. 8:19–20). The people pleaded with the prophet Samuel to find them a king like everyone else.

To the south, the Egyptian pharaohs were worshiped as semi-divine. Their achievements were memorialized by massive building projects which marvel even modern tourists. With their long history of godlike rule, the pharaohs gifted their people with confidence and a sense of stability that even the wandering Israel- ites, having just escaped Egyptian enslavement, found themselves drawn back into. To the west, the Philistines also had kings. The five great Philistine cities, with their kingly rulers, had quickly come to dominate the lowlands along the Mediterranean. Their kings helped usher in that technological revolution of iron. To the east, the Ammonites, Moabites, and Edomites all had kings, kings known for their ferocity in battle, kings like warring lions.

But Israel had no king, nothing that even resembled a king.

The closest thing they had was Samuel, a kind of roaming prophet, probably with a grayed beard and a homemade staff. Samuel was no deified pharaoh, no entrepreneurial Philistine, and no mighty Ammonite warrior. It's easy to imagine how the Israelites, little more than impoverished peasants, would have come to associate political power and material success with the image of a king. It was the common denominator of all the great nations around them. And so, the Israelites began to pray to God for their own—a king like all the other nations.

When we are first introduced to Saul, he was nothing more than a son out looking for his father's lost donkeys. Saul was empty-handed and without a plan. It was his servant who shrewdly guided him toward finding the animals. But Saul had two traits that the Bible makes explicitly clear: he was handsome and he was tall. Or, as it's put in 1 Samuel, "There was not a man among the people of Israel more handsome than he. From his shoulders upward he was taller than any of the people" (1 Sam. 9:2). We are suckers for leaders that look the part. In Hebrew, Saul's name translates to "the one asked for." The people took one look at him and were ready to hand him the crown.

Looks matter. A public image is a valuable thing. In an article entitled *Short Changed*, Steven Landsburg explained economically just how much it pays to be, particularly, tall. He wrote, "Multiple studies have found that an extra inch of height can be worth an extra $1,000 a year or so in wages, after controlling for education and experience. If you're 6 feet tall, you probably earn about $6,000 more than the equally qualified 5-foot-6-inch shrimp down the hall."[4]

The Princeton psychologist Alexander Todorov posed this same question as a scientific experiment. He decided to investigate what psychologist Nalini Ambady calls "thin-slice" judgment.[5] It's the idea that we form powerful social conclusions based on seconds-long observations of one another, things like height equals political competence.

Todorov set up an experiment in which he would show two unknown faces to a participant for a tenth of a second and then ask them to pick the face that appeared most competent, competence being routinely one of the most important characteristics voters say impact their decision between two political candidates. Todorov explained, "We never told our test subjects they were looking at candidates for political office—we only asked them to make a gut reaction response as to which unfamiliar face appeared more competent."[6] The results? By comparing the participants' choices with the actual outcome of the elections, test subjects were able to accurately predict the winning candidate in 72.4 percent of the year's races for US Senate and 68.8 percent of gubernatorial races.

Was it this same human tendency that made Saul so enticing to eager Israelites looking for a king? Long before peer-reviewed psychological experiments, the Bible recognized how much image shapes our interest. We base a lot on looks. First Samuel records the crowd's reaction to Saul's appearance. "'There is none like him among all the people.' And all the people shouted, 'Long live the king!'" (1 Sam. 10:24). Israel needed only a split second to recognize exactly what they had been looking for. Saul looked like a king; it was enough to make him one. Saul had his reputation and now the real work of trying to live up to it.

CLOTHING AND REPUTATION

Wisdom warns of confusing reputation and character. Thomas Paine explained, "Reputation is what men and women think of us; character is what God and angels know of us."[7] The American writer and philosopher Elbert Hubbard similarly expressed, "Many a man's reputation would not know his character if they met on the street."[8] But it was Mark Twain who captured it best: "Give a man a reputation as an early riser, and he can sleep 'til noon."[9]

Saul was catapulted from obscurity to royalty by little more than his appearance. His reputation was formed by little more than his stature. And his story was a constant struggle to be what he appeared to be. The crown, along with its expectations, became his curse, and his life began to unravel under its weight. To the world, he projected an image of power, control, and nobility, but within he was coming apart, torn apart by fits of jealousy, rage, and paranoia. Like that White House tree, his lack of integrity guaranteed his collapse.

That discrepancy between outward appearance and inner truth is a theme of Saul's and David's stories. It led to Saul's defeat, and though David was anointed by God, he too would have to wrestle with that age-old instinct to defend his reputation at the expense of his integrity and the truth of his own inner life. An over-identification with our public reputation is an instinct many men know and one to which many men have forfeited their integrity and the truth of their lives to keep.

The narrator of these biblical stories uses a thematic image to draw out this tension. Over and over, these men are characterized by the garments they are given and the garments they wear. The story is littered with descriptions of clothing. The prophet Samuel grew up wearing that simple linen ephod his mother sewed and replaced each year. Goliath lumbered onto the battlefield, defined by his snake-like suit of bronze. For David and Saul, the descriptions of their garments are central to almost every story.

In fact, the Hebrew language has long connected these two themes in ways not always obvious to the English reader. The Hebrew root *bagad* can be used as a noun for clothing and also as a verb to conceal and to deceive. English has some similar equivalents. To dress and to disguise are words with related roots, and a cloak can be both an outer garment and a verb meaning to hide. For ancient Hebrew readers, the relationship between the two would have been more tightly integrated.

Saul offered David his armor to face Goliath. Jonathan offered David his robe as a sign of friendship and David's right to the throne. David served as Saul's armor-bearer, responsible for his royal garments. David symbolically spared Saul's life but secretly cut away the hem of Saul's garment. Saul accidentally tore Samuel's robe, who took it as a sign that God would tear the kingdom away from Saul. David escaped Saul by laying clothes out on his bed as a disguise. Saul wore his own disguise to approach the witch at Endor, who saw through it. David's ambassadors were stripped of their clothes. David fled Jerusalem with his head uncovered and barefoot. David's daughter, Tamar, tore her royal robes and refused to pretend everything was okay. Was Bathsheba's nakedness on the roof, and David's taking her for himself, not an inversion of all the other garments offered to him throughout the story?

The list goes on and on. But I want to show you two of the most important examples: one from Saul and one from David.

NAKED SAUL, NAKED DAVID

Saul was determined to kill David and got word that David was staying with the prophet Samuel at a place called Ramah. Saul sent men to take David captive. But as they approached, they saw the great prophet Samuel and his company of prophets and Saul's men were overcome by the Spirit of the Lord. They began to prophesy. As they were caught up in this moment of worship, David was spared.

Saul must have been furious. It was bad enough the people were constantly singing about David. Bad enough, the rumors that Samuel had already anointed David the next king. Now his men were too busy playing prophet to carry out his orders. Saul sent a second detachment. They too were overcome by the Spirit, and so were Saul's third group of men. Finally, Saul decided to go himself.

As Saul approached, the Spirit came over him too. "He too stripped off his clothes, and he too prophesied before Samuel and lay naked all that day and all that night" (1 Sam. 19:24). David escaped; Saul lay on the ground exposed.

It's a strange story. The great king Saul naked and captive before the Spirit. But it's not hard to understand its significance. Saul is not stronger than the Lord. His royal robes and reputation are not reality. What is true is his nakedness. What's true, he cannot finally hide. The Spirit exposes him.

Walter Brueggeman explains it well in his commentary. "The pitifully embarrassing scene is that of this once great man, still tall but no longer great, exhausted by demanding religious exercise, clearly not in control, shamed, now rendered powerless in a posture of submissiveness. This episode is an act of dramatic de-legitimation of Saul."[10] Saul can wear all the robes he wants, parade before the people, boast of his achievements, give his commands, and rave in madness at his enemies, but we see him for what he is. A naked man forced to the ground before God's prophet. Saul's public reputation can't save him from the truth.

* * *

Later, after David became king, he began to solidify his power by moving his throne to Jerusalem. There, he began ambitious building projects: walls, palaces, and government buildings. The city also bore his name, the City of David, and David designed it as an image of his power and achievement. He also sought to consolidate Israel's religious focus within that city.

For some time, the ark had been kept at a place called Baalah. After it had been lost to the Philistines and miraculously returned, Israel wasn't quite sure what to do with it. David must have seen it as an opportunity. He gathered 30,000 men and went to bring the ark to Jerusalem. They constructed a special ox-drawn cart, loaded the ark, and kicked off a parade I've always imagined was something like Aladdin's entrance into Agrabah as Prince Ali.

It was a party with music and excitement and anticipation. The Bible sets David at the center of the festivities, celebrating as they went. The Bible doesn't depict it as a religious scene. The celebration is more closely connected to laughter, celebration, and entertainment. It's the same language used by the women singing about how David had killed his tens of thousands of Philistines. You get the feeling it's a kind of political rally around him.

Suddenly, one of the oxen stumbled, and the ark began to shift off the cart. One of the attendants reached up and steadied

THE 5 MASCULINE INSTINCTS

the ark, but at the moment his hand touched it, he was struck dead. It's not hard to imagine how the lightning strike of divine judgment might ruin the mood of the party. With a scratch of the vinyl, the music stopped, and eyes turned toward David. What would happen next?

The Bible tells us that David was angry and afraid—angry that his plans had been interrupted and afraid of the display of divine judgment which interrupted it. They ditched the ark in a nearby house and went home. Three months passed. Was David sulking, plotting, fuming? Embarrassed that God's judgment had tarnished his image as God's man? We don't know. But David eventually returned to the ark. His second attempt looked much different.

This time, instead of a cart, the ark would be carried by men, as God had commanded. And as they began, David halted them after just six steps to stop and offer a sacrifice to the Lord. This time David went before the ark dancing in a linen ephod. It was the common dress of a religious servant. It was the same humble garment Hannah had sewed for the boy Samuel. It was nothing special, but it was distinctly religious and humble. He led as a servant, not as a king.

As they came into the city, David's wife, Michal, the daughter of Saul, saw him. "She despised him in her heart" (2 Sam. 6:16). As David returned home, she berated him. "How the king of Israel honored himself today, uncovering himself today before the eyes of his servants' female servants, as one of the vulgar fellows shamelessly uncovers himself" (2 Sam. 6:20). She was mocking him. There is no mention of David actually exposing himself. The passage never says that he was naked, but that was her accusation. Michal, like her father, knew the importance of reputation and public image. What bothered her was the way David had presented himself, not as a king but as a servant. He had under-mined the social roles and the proper appearance of servants and masters. He had embarrassed himself by acting beneath his public reputation. As his wife, she felt the threat to her own image.

David and Saul both share this moment of being exposed. Saul's was forced on him by the Spirit. David had chosen to set aside his reputation to be humble before the Lord. Saul des-perately fought to hang on to the image and reputation of his throne. David was not immune to the temptation. Though here he seems to understand the lesson, the humility to be honest about who he really was—to recognize and own the truth beneath the public image—was something David would fail at as often as he got it right.

BLIND TO WHAT'S COMING

As men, we are notorious for our ability to ignore ninety per-cent of life and focus on the ten percent in which we are most competent, most capable of winning. We intuitively sense our weaknesses and hide them in an attempt at ignorance. We believe that success in business, or a certain hobby, or a certain physique is enough to define us, to give our life a meaningful presentation to the world. Knowing parts of ourselves are unaccounted for, we cope by refusing any personal introspection. We tell ourselves we're too practical for that kind of emotional mumbo-jumbo. We become less reflective, less vulnerable, less articulate about our-selves. We become less a person and more our persona. I think we do it mostly out of fear for what we know is there: the truth.

Most are familiar with the old story of the emperor who paraded before his kingdom without his clothes. The story goes that two weavers offered the king a remarkable robe which was invisible to those who were "hopelessly stupid" and unfit to recognize their value. After such a proclamation, no subject, nor the king himself, dared to admit they couldn't see them and, by so doing, expose their own deficiencies and inferiority. So, the king paraded naked while everyone believed his nudity was only a sign of their own inadequacy. Both leaders and followers pretended to be impressed by what they knew didn't exist, believing that to say so would only expose themselves. They all went along, pretending they didn't know what was actually there.

That image—the emperor with no clothes—has persisted because of its universal truth. Desperate not to expose ourselves, to protect what we imagine is a meaningful reputation, we walk around naked, unwilling to acknowledge what every human similarly experiences. We ignore our inner lives, we play dumb to what we know is there, and we hope, distracted by their own nakedness, no one will point out ours.

As a pastor, I sometimes get discouraged that the church has too often exacerbated a tendency to hide behind façades and cover up the truth of ourselves. Bonhoeffer wrote of the church, "Though they have fellowship with one another as believers and as devout people, they do not have fellowship as the undevout, as sinners. The pious fellowship permits no one to be a sinner. So everybody must conceal his sin from himself and from the fellowship. We dare not be sinners. Many Christians are unthinkably horrified when a real sinner is suddenly discovered among the righteous. So, we remain alone with our sin, living in lies and hypocrisy."[11]

We become divided men. Men living in two worlds. Men desperate to cover up our nakedness. We become only an image, propped up by our own pleasantries and smiles and concealed truth. Always doing fine. Hoping no one pries too deep. Men with hidden searching and erased histories. Men unable to talk about anything but external triviality. Eventually, our integrity compromised by avoiding the truth, we are prone to collapse. Like David, the duplicity is eventually exposed. Integrity is not a take-it-or-leave-it virtue. It is an inevitability, by choice or by fall. Who we really are always manages to get out.

As Søren Kierkegaard warned, "Don't you know that a midnight hour comes when everyone has to take off his mask? Do you think life always lets itself be trifled with? Do you think you can sneak off a little before midnight to escape this?"[12]

RETHINKING INTEGRITY

Integrity is often associated with ideas of honesty and faithfulness. A person with integrity, we imagine, would always do the right thing, even in the face of adversity. There is a common definition, variously attributed, that defines integrity as "doing the right thing even when no one is watching." It's this connotation of trustworthiness and certitude that makes integrity a favorite virtue of politicians, at least one that tends to show up every other fall.

Today's dictionaries demonstrate how we have diminished the virtue, defining integrity as merely possessing "strong moral principles." Integrity takes on connotations of Washington's cherry-tree convictions, a patina of Ol' Honest Abe. Integrity gets generalized into one more platitude for being a trustworthy fellow.

I think the older dictionaries capture more accurately the word's real significance, its radical challenge to our living. Webster's 1913 dictionary defines integrity as "the state or quality of being entire or complete; wholeness." It goes on to use the phrase "moral soundness,"[13] which sounds a lot like the engineer's talk of structural integrity or the arborist's conclusion about that deteriorating magnolia tree.

> A person of integrity is a person whose life is known and lived in full honesty, not always perfect but always accounted for.

Integrity is a word meant to describe an object's state of being whole. No rotted interior, no hidden deception. What a person appears to be is what they actually are. The word comes from the old Latin word for integer, a whole number. There are no fractions, no decimals, no extra parts, no moldy leftovers rotting in the back of the fridge. It is a tree with a solid trunk. A bridge with strong cables. A house without splintered joists hidden in the crawl space. What it claims to be, it is.

A person of integrity is a person whose life is known and lived in full honesty, not always perfect but always accounted for. It is a soul, fully inventoried, fully known, and fully integrated.

That is the nuance we too often miss. Integrity doesn't demand that we always do what is right, but rather that we are always honest, even about what we do wrong—a much more demanding call for truth. True integrity leaves no stone unturned, no shadow unexplored. Such integrity, which narrowly and wrongfully imagines itself as a simple outward honesty, claims to speak truthfully of only what is known, and so much of life—the real state of our souls, for instance—can be left intentionally unknown. We can manufacture a false sense of integrity by simply learning to avoid the more difficult parts of our own lives. We make our claim of integrity factoring in only what is publicly knowable.

But such a shallow view of integrity leaves the politician with only his slogans, the pastor covered by only his pulpit, and the businessman culpable for only the expectations printed on his business card. The compartments protect the truth from getting out. The compartments allow us to worship, witness, advise others, and go on living without the nagging guilt of what is also there. But such fractures eventually jeopardize our structural integrity. We are set for collapse but ignorant to the signs of it. As the apostle Paul pointed out, we paint the walls to cover up the crumbling stones.

Our lives are far from the wholeness demanded by the real virtue of integrity. To claim integrity is to claim to know the whole truth of who you are. It is an honest awareness and evaluation of your whole life. Might someone open the bag, reach in, and pull out absolutely any moment of your life and find it to be congruent with any other? Each of the pieces completing a single picture, and that picture, precisely the same you present to others and imagine of yourself?

It's a terrifying thought. It's terrifying because no matter how honest we imagine ourselves to be, our lives harbor all sorts of half-truths and incongruent secrets lurking in the shadows. Integrity demands courage, and when it comes to our own lives, pretending is so much easier and less demanding.

But you aren't alone. It was this same basic lack of integrity that collapsed David's life that day before the prophet Nathan. By God's revelation, Nathan pulled a scene from the uncatalogued portions of David's life and read it publicly. The weight of truth was set on the flimsy structure of David's self-erected public image. The structural integrity of that edifice cracked, splintered, and collapsed under the weight of the truth. David's life lacked the integrity to bear it. David appeared weak and defeated. He possessed the courage to battle giants but not to speak honestly of himself.

David's life might be the Bible's stiffest warning about the risks of ignoring your personal integrity. Live divided, and not only will you eventually be exposed, but you may not even see it coming. The life you were building may collapse on the very question of integrity you've been avoiding. The work of crafting your appearance and maintaining your reputation of integrity serves only to distract you from true deterioration and the inevitable fall.

We must build our lives around the truth. We have to deal with what is actually there. We can't ignore it. We can't hide it. God is too gracious to let us get away with that.

ACKNOWLEDGING THE INNER WOUND

Leo Tolstoy paints a remarkably insightful picture of how a person comes to be truly honest in his story *The Death of Ivan Ilych*. Tolstoy used the life of the fictitious Ivan to critique nineteenth-century Russian culture absorbed in the theatrics of social image and ostentatious appearance of wealth and influence. Ivan was cast as a governmental bureaucrat climbing the ladder of Russian society. Preoccupied with his career and maintaining the expected image of a person of wealth and prestige, Ivan paid increasingly less attention to who he really was. He became only the image that was expected of him. It was all a performance, one he both performed and was entertained by.

Tolstoy could have chosen to expose Ivan through some social unmasking. His marriage could have collapsed. His spending could have forced him into bankruptcy. He could have been caught in some salacious sin. But Tolstoy crafts a far simpler and more horrifying plot.

The literary move is brilliant. Tolstoy places the most critical scene of the story inside the privacy of Ivan's house, but not just in any room: in the drawing room, the most public room of the house in which he and his wife would have entertained guests. It was the most important room for putting on an appearance of wealth, class, and taste. In fact, Ivan had been overseeing a remodel of the house and that room. One day while climbing a ladder to demonstrate to the upholsterer just how the drapes should hang, Ivan slipped and "bumped his side on the knob of the window frame."[14]

It was nothing major—just a bruise. Ivan went about his business as usual. But from that day something in him began to ache. By all outward appearances, there was no injury, but Ivan became increasingly aware of a problem, an internal one. Tolstoy writes, "It could not be called ill health if Ivan Ilych sometimes said that he had a queer taste in his mouth and felt some discomfort in his left side. But this discomfort increased and, though not exactly painful, grew into a sense of pressure in his side accompanied by ill humor. And his irritability became worse and worse and began to mar the agreeable, easy, and correct life that had established itself."

Hopefully, you see why Tolstoy is one of my favorite writers. Ivan was sick. As a reader, we recognize that Tolstoy is pointing to a condition more universal than Ivan's damaged organ. We are all desperate to ignore the nagging damage within. Or as Tolstoy would put it, "The pain did not grow less, but Ivan Ilych made efforts to force himself to think that he was better. And he could do this so long as nothing agitated him. But as soon as he had any unpleasantness with his wife, any lack of success in his official work, or held bad cards at bridge, he was at once acutely sensible of his disease."[15]

Eventually, Ivan was forced to admit his condition, and he sensed that the inevitable outcome was death. As he struggled to grasp the reality of it, the layers of his deception began to fall away, and not just the lies about his disease, but also the lies about his life.

For Tolstoy, death was the ultimate reality, the great truth, that not even the wealthiest and most elite could finally hide from. No amount of opulence could glamorize the bare horror of it. Death forces each of us to contend with what is really there—we are not okay.

What I believe to be the most important line of the story comes in Ivan's own words just before his death. Ivan confesses, "It is as if I had been going downhill while I imagined I was going up. And that is really what it was. I was going up in public opinion, but to the same extent life was ebbing away from me. And now it is all done and there is only death."[16]

The final inescapable truth. Probably like yours, Ivan's story has far less dramatic flair than David's but the realization, the struggle for truth, is the same. Both are forced to admit that what is public is never really the full truth of who we are, that it is possible to appear one thing and be another. For Ivan Ilych, death is the tool by which he is finally able to find the integrity of truth, to escape the discrepancy of his pretending.

WHAT IS LEFT BUT TO CONFESS

Maybe the thing that is most remarkable about David's life is that we know so many of the lurid details. In our own day, politicians and leaders spend millions to cover up their sins. They hire attorneys, image consultants, and online reputation services to clean up any irregularity. But we know more about the life of David than any other character in the Bible or from the ancient world. It's all there: sin, failures, lies, cover-ups, consequences, and sorrow.

David's story is as uncomfortable and as messy as your own. In this way, David's story is all of our stories—the human story. It's this Davidic humanity that led Baruch Halpern to declare David "the first human being in world literature."[17] We know him because he came to know himself and to allow himself to be known.

Through David, we are reminded that the ultimate human question is not one of purpose, or achievement, or reputation; the fundamental human question is one of being. David's story, and ours, is a quest for truth. It is a question of wholeness and integrity. It is this honesty about himself that makes David's story so complicated, at times painful, and yet inspiring.

As Thomas Merton wrote, "There is something in the depths of our being that hungers for wholeness and finality. Because we are made for eternal life, we are made for an act that gathers up all the powers and capacities of our being and offers them simultaneously and forever to God."[18]

The book of 1 Kings records David's death. He had grown old and weak. The Bible records, "And although they covered him with clothes, he could not get warm" (1 Kings 1:1). He is fully human, in life and death. David is not remembered for the clothes that covered him nor the robes he wore. He is remembered for what he could confess. He is remembered for his integrity. And finally, he is remembered as a shivering and naked human, the truth of us all.

One of the last words of David's life is his confession, "When I kept silent, my bones wasted away through my groaning all day long. For day and night your hand was heavy on me; my strength was sapped as in the heat of summer. Then I acknowledged my sin to you and did not cover up my iniquity. I said, 'I will confess my transgressions to the LORD.' And you forgave the guilt of my sin" (Ps. 32:3–5 NIV).

G. K. Chesterton wrote that some think "it is morbid to confess your sins. I should say that the morbid thing is not to confess them. The morbid thing is to conceal your sins and let them eat your heart out, which is the happy state of most people in highly civilized communities."[19]

So much could and has been said about confession, but so much of it is an excuse for not doing it. It is not difficult to understand. It doesn't require special training or some monologue of memorized words. It only requires that you give up the game. You embrace what is there: the truth. With yourself. With God. With someone you trust. Confession is not ultimately about words; it is about a willingness to acknowledge what is. It is a willingness to open long shut doors to the light and grace of God. To be who you are before Him.

As Saint Augustine asked, "Would anything in me be secret even if I were unwilling to confess to you? I would be hiding you from myself, but not myself from you."[20] Stop hiding.

* * *

Recognize your instinct for reputation.
Recognize your need for honesty and integrity.

Chapter 7

APATHY: A WORLD TOO WIDE

THE ABRAHAM STORY: GENESIS 12–23

"If you stand still, you fall backwards. You cannot stand still, because the world moves away from you, if you stand still. There's no stasis; there's only backwards. And so, if you're not moving forwards, then you're moving backwards. Perhaps that's more of the underlying truth of the Matthew principle: 'to those who have everything, more will be given. From those who have nothing, everything will be taken.' It's a warning: do not stay in one place."

JORDAN PETERSON, *The Call to Abraham*

"The day men forget that love is synonymous with sacrifice, that day they will ask what selfish sort of woman it must have been who ruthlessly extracted tribute in the form of flowers, or what an avaricious creature she must have been who demanded solid gold in the form of a ring, just as they will ask what cruel kind of God is it who asks for sacrifice and self-denial."

ARCHBISHOP FULTON SHEEN

Scientists have a name for the way the world seems to be constantly more complicated. They call it entropy. It's actually a part of the second law of thermodynamics. Systems never decrease in complexity; they always expand toward maximum entropy, toward maximum chaos. Everything gets more complicated with time. Things don't come together; they fall apart.

It is true at the smallest molecular level, true of the constantly expanding universe itself, true of time, and true of our experience of life. Stephen Hawking explained, "The increase of disorder or entropy with time . . . distinguishes the past from the future, giving a direction to time."[1] The longer we live, the more we sense this trend toward chaos. Build a house, and it immediately begins to fall apart; buy a car, and it has already begun to rust; light a fire, and it rushes to burn itself out.

Man's story is often described as a campaign against this decay. We keep building, keep innovating, keep struggling to hold on to what we create. As the waves and winds of time endlessly erode our work, we fight to keep it. We call it—maybe too optimistically—progress.

What was it that drew those ancient builders to the plain of Shinar to stack their stones into a tower toward heaven? What compelled them to build cities and empires, to carve civilization from the dust? What caused them to place crowns on their heads and construct monuments to their own renown? Was their building not an attempt to overthrow the power of time and ultimate deterioration?

Eventually, even the worship of the gods took on this same goal of ordering the chaotic. Ancient shamans searched for the means of appeasing divine forces, practices of worship, which might allow them to exert control over the chaotic experiences of weather, war, and fertility. Still today, it is the promise of technology, supercomputers with mass data and algorithms frantically scouring the universe for patterns that promise new possibilities of control and conquest.

The science historian James Gleick writes, "Organisms organize. . . . We sort the mail, build sand castles, solve jigsaw puzzles, separate wheat from chaff, rearrange chess pieces, collect stamps, alphabetize books, create symmetry, compose sonnets and sonatas, and put our rooms in order. . . . Not only do living things lessen the disorder in their environments; they are in themselves, their skeletons and their flesh, vesicles and membranes, shells and carapaces, leaves and blossoms, circulatory systems and metabolic pathways—miracles of pattern and structure. It sometimes seems as if curbing entropy is our quixotic purpose in the universe."[2]

Is this ordering of the chaos what God meant when He called Adam to subdue and have dominion over creation? Was this God's work in calling forth light from the darkness of the primordial seas? Whatever that work was like in that first heavenly garden, our work is carried out in a universe of curse. Like Adam's would become, our work is done among thorn and thistle and only by the sweat of our brow. Weed the garden today, and tomorrow the bramble will be back. The harvest is an endless exertion of will over chaos. It's all so very exhausting.

It's also increasingly complicated and messy. There is always waste, always unintended consequences. What we order leaves a trail of disorder in its wake. There is always a hidden cost. There are no perfectly efficient machines. We make progress always at the expense of regression somewhere else. The longer we live, the more we recognize how true it is.

What is man left to do against this relentless deterioration? In *The Count of Monte Cristo*, Edmond Dantès offers the toast, "Life is a storm, my young friend. You will bask in the sunlight one moment, be shattered on the rocks the next. What makes you a man is what you do when that storm comes. You must look into that storm and shout. . . . Do your worst, for I will do mine. Then the fates will know you as we know you—as Albert Mondego, the man."[3]

I'm not convinced yelling into the storm makes much of a difference. That's a young man's game. Shakespeare described the final stage of man by depicting his change in voice. "His big manly voice, turning again towards childish treble, pipes and whistles in his sound."[4] There is no shout left to confront the storm. Only, as Shakespeare put it, "a world too wide" to go on pushing back against. As we age, as we feel the full weight of the world's complexity, the fight in us begins to dim. Our shout diminishes with it.

Entropy takes its toll not just on creation but on our energy to go on engaging the world's complexity. Having offered a lifetime of work and having mounted our best attempts to control it, we come to understand how little of life actually can be controlled. Things we build fall apart. Your life's work is erased by a single decision of your replacement. Problems you thought solved in youth resurface later in life. Society grows more perplexing and frustrating. Relationships seem to require more than they once paid back. Gradually we disengage. We content ourselves with little hobbies, little enclaves of control, little lives clutching at little comforts.

In their book *Growing Old*, social scientists Elaine Cumming and William Earl Henry described their theory of Social Disengagement in which the inevitability of death and the recognition of deteriorating abilities causes us to gradually and increasingly detach ourselves from the world.[5] We let go of what we can't control, and time only reveals how little we can.

A new instinct develops. We grow increasingly apathetic to the world outside of our control. Can't we just be left alone?

NOTHING LEFT BUT TO LAUGH

According to Mark Twain, "[The human race], in its poverty, has unquestionably one really effective weapon—laughter."[6]

Abraham was ninety-nine years old when he received the promise of a son. Having much earlier heard the call of God to go, Abraham had packed up his family and become a pilgrim in pursuit of God's better future. That long migration was not typical in ancient times. Most would live and die within the same few square miles of their birth. But Abraham wandered across horizons. He fought battles, negotiated with kings, survived famines, bore the pain of his wife's barrenness, and through all of it, earned a reputation for faith. Abraham is the archetypal character of faith. Faith, which the apostle Paul described as having credited his righteousness. Abraham's name became synonymous with faith.

> For too many of us, faith is a soft and clean word. The kind of word you're likely to find cross-stitched onto a kitchen hand towel.

For too many of us, faith is a soft and clean word. The kind of word you're likely to find cross-stitched onto a kitchen hand towel. It's more accurate once it has been dirtied up a little bit. Abraham's faith is not some subtle optimism that allowed him to travel through life's challenges on a cloud. His story has none of the clichés or gimmicks which too often accompany the word in our church circles. For Abraham, faith was the battle to go on believing, to keep himself engaged with the full complexities of calling and hope in the midst of a world that was constantly tearing apart what he had attempted to build.

At the center of this desperate fight for faith was a promise from God, a promise that Abraham would have a son, and that his son would become a nation more numerous than the stars. Abraham had been standing beneath the stars when God called him to look upward and receive that promise. How many times had Abraham slipped out of his childless tent to look again upon those same stars and wonder how it would be? God might as well have promised him the moon. The barrenness which plagued his wife Sarah made the promise of a child seem more painful with each passing day. Their turning gray made it seem more a joke than a promise.

There had been Lot, Abraham's nephew. Lot traveled with Abraham for some time, and as his closest kin, would have inherited Abraham's possessions. Lot was like a son, but their relationship had not gone as Abraham must have hoped. Eventually, Lot's obvious ambitions and the strain of their relationship made it necessary for them to separate. Lot had chosen the best of Abraham's land for himself and had taken up residence near Sodom. Learning of Sodom's coming destruction, Abraham had worked up all the courage he had to negotiate a chance for Lot's escape. Would God spare Sodom if just ten righteous people were within the city? God had agreed. But the next day, when Abraham caught sight of the rising smoke of Sodom, he was left to fear the worst. Lot had escaped by God's warning, but Genesis never recounts a reunion between Abraham and Lot. It's not clear if Abraham ever learned of Lot's survival and Lot seems uninterested in preserving his relationship with Abraham, even as Abraham had loved him like a son and interceded on his behalf. Theirs was a complicated relationship.

There had also been Ishmael. Tired of waiting on God's

promise for a son, Sarah had contrived a plan to produce an heir through her Egyptian servant Hagar. Abraham passively went along with the plan, and Ishmael was born to Hagar. The plan produced a son, but it also produced more complexity and pain. Sarah despised Hagar for her ability to conceive. Abraham struggled to deal with the discord. He told Sarah to deal with it. So, Sarah "dealt harshly" with Hagar, and Hagar fled into the wilderness (Gen. 16:6).

At ninety-nine years of age, Abraham must have been tired. Sarah described herself as worn out. They had traveled so many miles, faced so many challenges, and borne so many disappointments and heartaches. So, what did Abraham do when, at ninety-nine, God spoke to him again and told him that Sarah would not remain barren but would still bear him a son? Abraham laughed. He fell facedown and began to laugh, asking himself, "Shall a child be born to a man who is a hundred years old?" (Gen. 17:17).

God went on, "Your wife shall bear you a son, and you shall call his name Isaac" (Gen. 17:19). In Hebrew, Isaac's name means laughter. God would take the incredulous laughter of Abraham's disbelief and turn it into a laughter of joy, a laughter of fulfillment.

Laughter is always a response—a by-product. It's never the first act but a reply. We laugh because of something which strikes us as ironic or unexpected. So, laughter requires some form of engagement with the world and its unpredictable ways. We can fake a laugh, laugh out of sarcasm, laugh at someone else's expense, but real laughter always involves surprise and participation. Theologian Reinhold Niebuhr explained, "Humor is, in fact, a prelude to faith; and laughter is the beginning of prayer."[7] Abraham's laughter at God's prediction did just that: it raised a possibility which he couldn't fully believe. It forced him into a test: faith or despair. Laughter gave way to prayer. "God, could it be that you would still work?"

There is a medieval Christian tradition in which priests would incorporate jokes into their Easter sermons to inspire laughter from their congregation. It was meant to serve as a reminder to the congregation of the way in which God had tricked Satan through the cross. The laughter was a way of participating in the unexpected ways of God. The joke was a pastoral tool to prod people into engaging this new resurrection reality.

A faith which can no longer laugh too often signals a faith that has been emptied of life, a faith apathetic and a hope too small.

TWO DITCHES

There has been some research that suggests that as we age, we laugh less.[8] Do we become more serious or just less amused by life? Though this trend toward apathy and disengagement is often associated with age, I see it impacting men of every age. An inability to cope with the complexity of life, the collapse of confidence in our own control, the disappointment of dashed dreams, and a deepening pessimism has led many men to withdraw from life and exist only in their smallest interests.

> I know far more men who have lost the vitality of their faith to the obsession of their hobbies and the security of their recliners than to the grotesque sins of violence or lust.

When we imagine the great threats to our lives, rarely does

apathy make the list. We imagine that what threatens our lives, and our faith, are those grand conflicts of tyranny and temptation—that great war of good versus evil and our being lured toward the dark side. We imagine that the greatest threat to our self-control is having it taken from us or being tricked out of it; we rarely recognize that the real threat is that we too often forfeit it to apathy. It need not be the grand sins that rob us of faith. If little pleasures and trivial diversions can stunt belief, all the easier.

As C. S. Lewis wisely warned, "Murder is no better than cards if cards can do the trick. Indeed the safest road to Hell is the gradual one—the gentle slope, soft underfoot, without sudden turnings, without milestones, without signposts."[9]

I know far more men who have lost the vitality of their faith to the obsession of their hobbies and the security of their recliners than to the grotesque sins of violence or lust.

In Neil Postman's book *Amusing Ourselves to Death*, he examined two dystopian views of the future, arguing that the one we worry least about is probably the more insidious. Postman compared two novels, George Orwell's *1984* in which an authoritarian government oppresses and controls society through power, and Aldous Huxley's *A Brave New World* in which citizens are instead controlled by pleasure and appetite. Postman wrote:

> What Orwell feared were those who would ban books. What Huxley feared was that there would be no reason to ban a book, for there would be no one who wanted to read one. Orwell feared those who would deprive us of information. Huxley feared those who would give us so much that we would be reduced to passivity and egoism. Orwell feared that the truth would be concealed from us. Huxley feared the

truth would be drowned in a sea of irrelevance. Orwell feared we would become a captive culture. Huxley feared we would become a trivial culture. . . . In *1984* . . . people are controlled by inflicting pain. In *Brave New World*, they are controlled by inflicting pleasure. In short, Orwell feared that what we hate will ruin us. Huxley feared that what we love will ruin us.[10]

That temptation is not modern; the Bible is awash in it. Adam passively took the forbidden fruit from Eve's hand. Noah, fresh off the ark and fresh into the sunlight of salvation, planted a vineyard, made wine, and passed out drunk and naked in his tent. Abraham acquiesced to Sarah's plan with Hagar. Isaac became known for his gullibility of character. Jacob was led into deception by his mother. Esau traded his birthright for a bowl of hot stew. Barak turned pale at the thought of battle. Jonah set sail for Tarshish to avoid Nineveh. David lounged on the roof while the other kings went out to war. Israel settled for a fraction of the land that had been promised them. The Bible offers as many passive men as it does aggressive ones.

We find ourselves in a cultural moment in which society seems to be most concerned about masculine aggression. In its controversial 2018 study, the American Psychological Association warned about the correlation between masculine stereotypes of aggression and the experience of masculine violence seen in bullying, assaults, and physical and verbal aggression. They saw the fundamental challenge of masculinity as unchecked masculine aggression. They called for society to address "social norms condoning male dominance and violence."[11]

There's no disputing the dangers of unchecked aggression, and it is too often a practice of men, but as an old Irish proverb states,

"For every mile of road, there are two miles of ditches." Avoiding aggression doesn't guarantee a man virtue. In fact, every new driver behind the wheel is warned that the real risk is an overcorrection. Attempting to avoid one ditch, you end up in the other.

Men produce destruction by more than violence. To warn only of man's aggression is to imply that passivity makes him safe and virtuous. Nothing could be further from the truth. As Agatha Christie warned, "A weak man in a corner is more dangerous than a strong man."[12] I'm convinced that disengagement and apathy produce more destruction in the lives of men than aggression and violence. One captures most of the national headlines, but it's the other that lays waste to homes and families all over the nation. Men must be warned of the danger of both ditches.

OLD MAN SKYWALKER

I grew up watching Star Wars. I was obsessed. And when my son was born, I couldn't wait to introduce him to the series. He was as hooked as I was, and we both anxiously waited for the release of J. J. Abrams' *The Force Awakens* and Rian Johnson's *The Last Jedi*. My son loved them; I struggled with the new plots and the changes to my once favorite characters. I wasn't alone.

Participating in the movie's publicity interviews, Mark Hamill stirred up plenty of controversy when describing his return to the character of Luke Skywalker. He told one reporter, bluntly, "He's not my Luke Skywalker."[13] Hamill was disappointed with the movie's take on Skywalker's later years. Once the hero of the original trilogy, this new Star Wars series depicted Skywalker as frustrated, calloused, and hiding on a deserted planet, unwilling to fight, unwilling to speak of any Jedi cause, and unwilling to engage the reawakening empire. The old man Skywalker seemed to be hiding in his basement.

Hamill explained, "I said 'Jedis don't give up.' I mean, even if he had a problem, he would maybe take a year to try and regroup, but if he made a mistake he would try and right that wrong, so right there, we had a fundamental difference, but, it's not my story anymore. It's somebody else's story."[14]

The comments sparked an explosion of fan reactions, expressed by a hashtag, #notmyluke. It was hard for many to see the once optimistic hero of their youth turned into yet another bitter and jaded old man. Hamill eventually walked back his comments, but I think he gave away more than he realized. This wasn't just about Luke Skywalker's character; it was about Hamill himself and, in so many ways, all of us.

Our stories do become someone else's. Battles we thought we won turn out to be less decisive than we imagined. Heroes are soon forgotten as new heroes emerge and old heroics are later revealed to have been more complicated than the original story told. We fight for our place in the story but end up looking only desperate against the tide of time. Eventually, it's too much. It's no longer our story. We complain for a while and then eventually succumb to a quiet bitterness.

I think the director's take on the aged Skywalker is more realistic than any of us would like to admit. We retreat. We stop laughing. We give up. We content ourselves with only what we can control. Faith gives way to apathy. Faith becomes only a doctrine, a membership card in our back pocket. The best we can imagine is just being left alone. We give in to the instinct of apathy.

BENEATH THE TAMARISK TREE

Isaac was eventually born. Though God's promise had strained Abraham's faith toward absurdity, Abraham's faith didn't fail him. He believed and received. He had everything he had imagined. The promised son was finally born, and both Abraham and Sarah laughed with joy. How Abraham must have looked at those same old stars, now with the sound of a child's laughter behind him in his tent.

Genesis tells us that Abraham was rich with livestock and land. Abraham had managed to sign treaties with many of his neighbors, ushering in a period of peace. There had been challenges and conflict, but most of it had now settled down. Hagar and Ishmael were gone, God having shown them far more compassion than Abraham and Sarah ever did. Lot was on his own. As tough as those decisions had been, things were now at least simpler and quieter.

Genesis records, "Abraham planted a tamarisk tree in Beersheba and called there on the name of the LORD, the Everlasting God. And Abraham sojourned many days" (Gen. 21:33–34). That tree was a testament, a milestone, a monument. And the verse seems to be a concluding transition from the life of Abraham, old and full of faith-filled laughter, to this new son and heir of the promises of God. Abraham had arrived. He was finally settled in the land God had promised, Beersheba, with its well of cool water to drink from. He had prospered in his work and faith. Now, over one hundred years old, Abraham's story draws to a close. All the promises fulfilled. Nothing left but to enjoy all that had been given, maybe even some grandkids in the years to come. We expect to turn the page and continue the Genesis story with Isaac at its center.

But things do not resolve so neatly for Abraham. They don't for us either. Immediately, we read, "After these things God tested Abraham" (Gen. 22:1).

THE PROGRESS OF MAN

A common modern myth is that man is progressing, that our acquisition of knowledge has allowed us to evolve into something more than we used to be. This myth has captured the way we think of society and politics, but it equally captures the way we think of our own individual achievements. A lifetime spent learning lessons and acquiring skills leaves us thinking we have achieved something, become something. What is life if not a trajectory toward better things? Surely, we do get better. Surely, we have improved ourselves.

The philosopher John Gray isn't convinced of our progress. He writes, "If there is anything unique about the human animal it is that it has the ability to grow knowledge at an accelerating rate while being chronically incapable of learning from experience."[15] Elsewhere, Gray has drawn a correlation between the increase of human knowledge and the increase in human irrationality. Having mapped the human genome, planted an American flag on the moon, and now possessing a universe of knowledge that fits in our pockets, we have still not solved the real pressing conditions of humanity: sorrow, loss, insecurity, pain, and sin. Is there progress if the same besetting sins of Abraham are still also ours?

Abraham's story is not an accumulation of faith that builds towards that final remarkable example of its accomplishment. The test Abraham finally faced challenged his entire understanding of faith and any sense of progress. Could everything that was gained be so quickly lost, sacrificed?

The promise that had for so long sustained him—the promise of a son—would be put to the test. What he had hoped for, he would now be called to sacrifice. This test would not question what he had accumulated but would strip him of every accomplishment. It was progress itself put to the test.

It was unnerving, particularly at Abraham's age. Had he not proved enough? Again, Gray reminds us that this is the genius of the Genesis story. It won't let us imagine that time alone somehow exempts us from such challenges. Gray writes, "In comparison with the Genesis myth, the modern myth in which humanity is marching to a better future is mere superstition. . . . The message of Genesis is that in the most vital areas of human life there can be no progress, only an unending struggle with our own nature."[16] Neither age nor previous achievements exempt us from such things.

THE DREADED AMBIGUITY OF A TEST

God commanded Abraham, "Take your son, your only son Isaac, whom you love, and go to the land of Moriah, and offer him there as a burnt offering on one of the mountains of which I shall tell you" (Gen. 22:2). At first read, there is little room for ambiguity. Abraham had two options: obey or disobey. Make the sacrifice or refuse. It is terrifying, and for generations, commentators have struggled to contend with the implications of this divine command.

When we think of tests, we imagine those marked-up pages with the grade circled in red pen at the top margin. We bring with us that image of a test when we read that God was now testing Abraham. What grade would Abraham receive?

Though most of us hope to get these tests over with as quickly as possible, the real purpose of a test is always more than a grade. A test reveals what can be too easily assumed. A teacher, having lectured, can't guarantee that the students have been paying attention. They can't assume they have even been heard. A test exposes what is there and what isn't. A test reveals what is true.

Abraham's test was not simply true or false; it was far more complicated than that. The simplicity of God's command left endless room for the truth of Abraham's life to form its own answer. Might he negotiate as he had for Lot? Might he scheme with Sarah for some clever loophole? Could he find some way out of it, or should he mindlessly obey? What Abraham could not do was be apathetic. The test forced him to act.

Abraham's task seems obvious to us. Take your son and kill him. Prove yourself faithful. But commentators have long recognized an uneasy ambiguity in God's choice of words. At the center of the ambiguity is God's command to offer Isaac as an *olah*. The Hebrew word has a broad range of meaning, anywhere from the general sense of 'going up' to the more specifically described process of offering a whole burnt offering. Though the word became technically defined in the book of Leviticus, in the Genesis stories it is rare and only used once before God's command to Abraham.

The question is, was God asking Abraham to prepare Isaac, to bring Isaac up to the place of sacrifice, or to offer him as a burnt offering? And how did Abraham understand the command? That ambiguity may be the point. Abraham was forced into decision. Many historic Jewish commentators have seen in this ambiguity a larger test. Rashi, writing during the medieval period, commented, "[God] did not say, 'Slay him,' because the Holy One, blessed be He, did not desire that he should slay him, but he told him to bring him up to the mountain to prepare him as a burnt offering."[17] How far would that preparation go?

We aren't given any clues to Abraham's thinking. His words and actions form a seemingly unreconcilable contradiction. He moves without protest towards the task. Three days' journey—time enough to ponder every other possibility. Yet, he rose early, took the knife and the wood, and led his son up the mountain. He bound Isaac, placed him on the wood of the altar, and lifted the sacrificial knife. He was unflinching. His action is deliberate and without hesitation.

But was this what Abraham had expected? He had commanded his servants to wait until he and Isaac returned from the mountain. How would Isaac return if slaughtered? When Isaac asked about the animal they would sacrifice, Abraham told him, "God will provide for himself the lamb for the *olah*, my son" (Gen. 22:8). Did Abraham believe God would provide a lamb, or was his answer only appeasement to Isaac's curiosity?

The most striking detail of the story is what is missing. Just at the moment of sacrifice and the knife's plunge, the angel stayed Abraham's hand. Abraham looked up and discovered a ram caught in a nearby thicket. Genesis records, "And Abraham went and took the ram and offered it up as a burnt offering instead of his son" (Gen. 22:13).

What is missing from the story is surprise. Imagine the relief of Abraham, that at the last moment he was spared the obligation of forcing that knife into his son's body. Imagine the relief of Isaac, who perhaps had finally understood his father's plans.

Eugene Peterson writes: "Not a word of surprise, not a single emotion of surprise in the story as written. Why am I surprised and Abraham and Isaac are not? Here is what I think: The *Akedah* was a three-day journey for Abraham, but it cannot be understood apart from a hundred years of road-tested faith that comprises the Abraham story."[18]

What is this clarity of faith that allows Abraham to act in the midst of such overwhelming conflict? The author of the book of Hebrews answered, "By faith Abraham, when he was tested, offered up Isaac. . . . He considered that God was able even to raise him from the dead, from which, figuratively speaking, he did receive him back" (Heb. 11:17–19).

I find that word "even" fascinating. It implies not a simple yes-or-no situation, but a spectrum. Abraham anticipated so many ways God could work, *even* resurrection. Abraham was prepared to act not knowing at what point on that spectrum the test would be passed.

So much could be and has been said about Abraham's sacrifice. Kierkegaard rightly described it as a story of profound fear and trembling. In many ways, it is a story only cheapened and diminished by any simple explanation, but this much is forever obvious: Abraham is not a character of disengaged apathy. Not old age nor the weathering crucible of divine ambiguity could erode his resolve. Abraham acts. By faith. God's command pulls him out of his apathy and forces him into a world of engagement where faith alone can find a way.

His faith is not simply a doctrinal position, nor is it a distant memory of some youthful repentance. His faith keeps him in it—in the complexity and mystery of life, living and acting before God. Faith propels him decisively into the ambiguity. This test was never about a grade but about the possibility of living what he had long believed. It was an opportunity to receive an even greater testimony of God's faithfulness.

APATHY: A WORLD TOO WIDE

AN ENDLESS (LIVING) SACRIFICE

As men, we are stereotypically obsessed with being in control. There are the obvious tropes: men refuse to ask for directions, refuse to read the instructions, and refuse to let anyone else operate the remote. But the problem runs much deeper. We fear what we can't control, can't conquer, can't beat. We refuse the test we can't pass. If we can't control it, we don't want anything to do with it. If we can't win, we'd rather not play the game.

Maybe it's this fear which begins to shallow out our faith. Knowing that faith implies ambiguity and ambiguity implies a complexity outside of our control, we balk. We want faith to be something we simply sign in agreement, not something that is put to the test. But biblically, faith is always proved through sacrifice. Faith must let go as easily as it hangs on. As Peterson put it, "The test is conducted by means of sacrifice."[19] It is always this way.

> Sacrifice forces us out of our complacency and apathy in ways receiving tends not to. It doesn't require action to wish for something, but faith that can be tested is willing to make the sacrifice.

In fact, it is best this way. The greatest evidence of faith is not what we receive but what we can afford to lose. Sacrifice forces us out of our complacency and apathy in ways receiving tends not to. It doesn't require action to wish for something, but faith that can be tested is willing to make the sacrifice.

To avoid sacrifice is to starve faith, leaving it not only weak but often lost entirely. C. S. Lewis made the same warning in describing the risk and complexity of love. He explained,

> To love at all is to be vulnerable. Love anything, and your heart will certainly be wrung and possibly be broken. If you want to make sure of keeping it intact, you must give your heart to no one, not even to an animal. Wrap it carefully round with hobbies and little luxuries; avoid all entanglements; lock it up safe in the casket or coffin of your selfishness. But in that casket—safe, dark, motionless, airless—it will change. It will not be broken; it will become unbreakable, impenetrable, irredeemable.[20]

Vulnerability always comes with the temptation to recoil, to disengage, and to distract ourselves from the risk. In the end, this reluctance costs everything. Even psychoanalyst Carl Jung understood that at the center of self-possession and engagement is the necessity of sacrifice. He wrote, "Sacrifice proves that you possess yourself, for it does not mean just letting yourself be passively taken: it is a conscious and deliberate self-surrender, which proves that you have full control of yourself."[21] In refusing to make the sacrifice, you expose your own desperation and fragile control. Only a man who by the virtue of faith truly possesses himself can willingly lay himself down. Everyone else clings desperately for control.

Following God is not a gradual trajectory toward comfort and retirement. Often, the tests of sacrifice increase. More is asked of us. Just when we're ready to put our feet up and take the load off, he asks us to sacrifice that hard-earned possibility of ease. He does this not to frustrate us but to free us, to keep us living. Left to our own instinct for apathy, we disengage and risk the very things we care most about. The test forces us back into life; it forces us back into our truest self. Left to our own way, we die long before our bodies do.

This is what so many have failed to understand about Abraham's test. In *The God Delusion,* Richard Dawkins wrote, "God ordered Abraham to make a burnt offering of his longed-for son. Abraham built an altar, put firewood upon it, and trussed Isaac up on top of the wood. His murdering knife was already in his hand when an angel dramatically intervened with the news of a last-minute change of plan: God was only joking after all, 'tempting' Abraham, and testing his faith. . . . By the standards of modern morality, this disgraceful story is an example simultaneously of child abuse, bullying in two asymmetrical power relationships, and the first recorded use of the Nuremberg defence: 'I was only obeying orders.'"[22]

Dawkins is right about one thing: humanity is quick to claim we were only obeying orders, but what Dawkins misunderstands is that it is far more often disengaged apathy which claims the Nuremberg defense than it is those men desperate to make the necessary sacrifices to stay alive to God.

What Dawkins was referring to—the Nuremburg defense—was a common position taken by German officers arrested and tried for their participation in the Nazi concentration camps. In 2018 the movie "Operation Finale" told the true story of a secret Israeli operation to capture Adolf Eichmann, a former SS officer and organizer of the Final Solution, the plan used by the German government to capture and execute more than six million Jews.

The movie is suspenseful and action-packed: disguises, secret plots, undercover espionage, and the risk of violent defeat. But maybe the best part is the depiction of Eichmann himself. As the movie unfolds, the appalling image of a man credited with millions of murders gives way to the unremarkable image of a mere human, one which must be fed, shaved, and regularly led to the toilet by his captors—blind without his glasses. Scene by scene, Eichmann becomes more human, less the animal he is said to be.

The realization that one of the century's most grotesque villains was actually a quite normal person need not diminish the man's guilt. His humanity isn't a defense. It suggests something far more uncomfortable. The most horrific acts of evil can be carried out by people indiscernibly similar to you and me. Far from an animal, Eichmann was a boring bureaucrat who justified horrific evil as simply carrying out orders. It's this blind and thoughtless loyalty that Dawkins reads into Abraham.

I think the movie may have actually made Eichmann more interesting than he really was; you know the way Hollywood casting always ends up with characters more attractive and articulate than their historical realities. Judging from historical photos and trial videos, Eichmann seems more like someone you would encounter at the DMV than leading a Nazi death squad.

In 1961, Hannah Arendt, a European Jew who had barely managed to escape the concentration camps herself, was sent on assignment by *The New Yorker* to cover Eichmann's trial in Jerusalem. Arendt made the same observation the movie's producers sought to capture. Eichmann was far less impressive than his reputation.

Arendt coined the phrase the "banality of evil." You can define banal as "so lacking in originality as to be obvious and boring." What Arendt observed was that evil feeds not just on extremism, but just as frequently on our apathy. Sin works its way deepest into the most boring and passive lives. Arendt wrote,

"The sad truth of the matter is that most evil is done by people who never made up their minds to be or do either evil or good."[23]

Apathy is not dangerous because of its lack of action; it's dangerous because, having neglected the testing of faith, it becomes banal and unable, or maybe unwilling, to distinguish between what is good and evil. It becomes unable to act at all.

This is what Dawkins misses in the Abraham story. The real danger is not that Abraham would sacrifice his son; the real risk is that, having had all his desires fulfilled, he might contract from faith and slip into a position of defensiveness which distorts not only who he is but also his disposition towards the world. Clutch too tightly at anything, and you risk shattering it. For Abraham the real risk was always apathy.

God would not allow Abraham to become a mindless bureaucrat of faith. His forcing Abraham to act keeps him discerning good and evil in ways apathy and comfort only obscure. Consider not just the horror of the test but what emerges from the story itself: Abraham's trust in God is demonstrated to himself, to Isaac, and to all those who would follow in his faith. Abraham would experience the gift of receiving his son for a second time. Isaac's identity was no longer defined exclusively by the promise to his father; he had witnessed his own deliverance first-hand. There would be no mistaking for future generations that God would not require a child's life for any father's sacrifice. And maybe most importantly, that place of deliverance would forever be remembered as "on the mount of the LORD it shall be provided" (Gen. 22:14).

There is a long tradition that connects the mountain of Abraham's testing with the future city of Jerusalem's temple and not far from the place of Jesus' sacrifice at Golgotha. And so that place became a monument to faith. Not just to Abraham, but to all who would look ahead to what God would do, engaging their own complex times and by faith acting and living their way into them.

The apostle James would later write, "Count it all joy, my brothers, when you meet trials of various kinds, for you know that the testing of your faith produces steadfastness" (James 1:2–3). Steadfastness has a unique sense of sustaining the weight of a heavy load. It is a particular form of strength. Don't despise the test. There is no end. Each moment of faith is both an arrival and an invitation to more, for all eternity; glory upon glory.

A SACRIFICE UNSEEN

Often the tests of faith we face are not nearly as dramatic as Abraham's. Usually, our sacrifices seem so much smaller, but that doesn't make them easier. Sometimes it's the littlest sacrifices—unnoticed, undramatic, and seemingly inconsequential—that are the hardest to make. But I'm convinced the risks are the same. It was never Isaac's life that was really at stake; it was always Abraham's life of faith.

Peterson makes the point well:

> The way of Abraham continues today along these same lines. Somewhere along the way we realize that we are not in charge of our own lives. . . . We enter the lifelong process of no longer arranging the world and the people on our terms. We embrace what is given to us—people, spouse, children, forests, weather, city—just as they are given to us, and sit and stare, look and listen until we begin to see and hear the

God-dimensions in each gift, and engage with what God has given, with what he is doing. Every time we set out, leaving our self-defined or culture-defined state, leaving behind our partial and immature projects, a wider vista opens up before us, a landscape larger with promise.[24]

The greatest risk to your faith probably isn't you abandoning it but that it would grow lifeless and still as you find ways to escape the complexity of what you currently face. The sacrifices you want to avoid are the gifts you most need. The sacrifice never actually costs you; it always opens the door to a bigger world. It stretches you and equips you with a greater capacity to receive from God. To sacrifice is to live. And it's always worth it.

> **Sometimes it's the littlest sacrifices–unnoticed, undramatic, and seemingly inconsequential–that are the hardest to make. But I'm convinced the risks are the same.**

* * *

Recognize your instinct for apathy.
Recognize your need for sacrifice.

Chapter 8

THE REAL WORK AHEAD

"A strong and well-constituted man digests his experiences (deeds and misdeeds all included) just as he digests his meats, even when he has some tough morsels to swallow."

FRIEDRICH NIETZSCHE

"There are [those] who never learn to see anything except in its relation to themselves, nor that relation except as fancied by themselves; and, this being a withering habit of mind, they keep growing drier, and older, and smaller, and deader, the longer they live—thinking less of other people, and more of themselves and their past experience, all the time as they go on withering."

GEORGE MACDONALD

Ernest Gordon realized his chances of survival were slim. He had been captured along with a group of British officers on a fishing boat they had stolen in an attempted escape from Singapore. Gordon was placed in one of the harshest Japanese work camps of the Second World War. The camp used its prisoners to construct the Burma railway, leaving in its wake a trail of death, disease, and broken men.

But that endless physical toil was only a part of the camp's difficulty. The men were beaten, starved, and tortured physically but also psychologically. Gordon, who ultimately survived, later wrote, "As conditions steadily worsened, as starvation, exhaustion and disease took an ever-growing toll, the atmosphere in which we lived became poisoned by selfishness, hate, and fear. We were slipping rapidly down the slope of degradation."[1]

Gordon described how a desperate instinct to survive began to infect them with hatred and strife, even among one another. "Existence had become so miserable, the odds so heavy against survival, that, to most of the prisoners, nothing mattered except to survive. We lived by the law of the jungle, 'red in tooth and claw'—the law of the survival of the fittest. It was a case of 'I look out for myself and to hell with everyone else.'"[2]

The power of the human will to survive makes for riveting stories. We love to hear how men, pressed to the edge of existence, battle nature and enemy to defeat the seemingly inevitable, like those stories of men adrift for months at sea or others who cut off a limb to escape being trapped beneath boulders.

Gordon's picture of survival is more honest, though. Surviving became animalistic. There were no heroes, no victors. Gordon admitted, "Everyone was his own keeper. It was free enterprise at its worst, with all the restraints of morality gone.[3] He also described it as, "men kicking their [friends] in the teeth when they're down; stealing from the dying; crawling like rats to the Japs."[4] They abandoned morality and lived by the instinct to survive.

But Gordon came to faith in that godless camp. In fact, many men did. Stories began to spread of a different kind of defiance. Gordon wrote, "There was a movement, a stirring in our midst, a presence."[5]

There's a story told in *Through the Valley of the Kwai*, Gordon's autobiographical account of survival, that has always stood out to me. The men were returning from a day's work, and as usual, made to stand at attention until their supplies had been properly returned and accounted for. This time a shovel was missing.

The commanding Japanese officer became irate, demanding that the stolen shovel be returned immediately. With no one confessing to the crime, the officer threatened to execute the entire unit. Finally, a single man stepped forward. The officer rushed forward and brought the butt of his rifle down on the man's head. He fell lifeless to the ground, dead. Just as the men were dismissed, word came that there had been an error in the count. There had never been a missing shovel.[6]

In a world in which every possible effort had been taken to rob them of dignity and meaning, in a camp where survival depended on self-interest alone, and where they lived among the constant cursing of life itself, what freed a man to do that? What allowed him to overcome even the instinct to survive for the sake of something beyond himself—to die for those who would happily have picked his pockets to save themselves?

WHAT THIS BOOK IS REALLY ABOUT

You are most likely not reading this book in a prison camp fighting for your survival and humanity. The conditions of your day pale in comparison, but the challenge to rise above the atmosphere of self-interest, to mature into something more than just your instincts, is no less a challenge. For the same sin which darkens a man's moments of blackest desperation are just as inwardly present on his days of peaceful rest. The willingness to live beyond yourself doesn't suddenly appear when you're pressed against the fence.

If, and when, that moment of desperation arises, you stand little chance of passing its test without having spent a life cultivating the maturity to act beyond your instincts. Without having matured to recognize your instincts and how to counterbalance them by faith, you will act by their logic and remain trapped by their demands.

Sarcasm will leave you immature and constantly offended. Adventure will leave you restless and ripe for betrayal. Ambition will leave you exhausted from its demand for more and its endless blaming of others. Reputation will hollow out your soul and leave your façade vulnerable to collapse. And apathy will lead you to disengagement as life is drained away. You must counter their power. You must question their authority. You must mature the instinct into something better.

> If, and when, that moment of desperation arises, you stand little chance of passing its test without having spent a life cultivating the maturity to act beyond your instincts.

That work begins this moment, even as we come to the end of this book. You have work to do. As George MacDonald put it, "I learned that he that will be a hero, will barely be a man; that he that will be nothing but a doer of his work, is sure of his manhood."[7] There is nothing heroic about this work. I imagine most people won't have any clue what you've undertaken. They won't offer you awards or promotions. It won't earn you a bigger paycheck. But few things could be more important. And few things are more rewarding than learning to discover a world beyond your own instincts—a world of Christ's better way.

That work is more important than this book. The truth is, you can forget about this book. You can toss it in the garbage and forget all of the instincts I've tried to describe. Maybe none fit you. But this book has always been about more than just those five masculine instincts. It's been about the process. It's been about you learning to think more deeply about your life and acquiring the character necessary to counterbalance your instincts with the truth of the gospel. That you can't afford to forget.

It has always been about those words Paul gave to Timothy, "Keep a close watch on yourself and on the teaching" (1 Tim. 4:16). That is how you too make progress. That is the work ahead of you.

WATCH YOUR LIFE

I can't impress upon you enough how important and neglected this work of watching your life really is. Honest self-knowledge may be the most lacking bit of information in our supposed age of it. We have the world's knowledge at our fingertips and yet become less and less articulate of the things within us.

The impulse to ignore self-knowledge is not the by-product of social media or endless online streaming. It has long been the compulsion of sinful man to ignore what he wants desperately not to know. The Puritan writer John Owen explains,

> Many men live in the dark to themselves all their days; whatever else they know, they know not themselves. They know their outward estates, how rich they are, and the condition of their bodies as to health and sickness they are careful to examine; but as to their inward man, and their principles as to God and eternity, they know little or nothing of themselves. Indeed, few labour to grow wise in this matter, few study themselves as they ought, are acquainted with the evils of their own hearts as they ought; on which yet the whole

course of their obedience, and consequently of their eternal condition, doth depend.[8]

You must learn to watch your life. If I've accomplished nothing else in this book but to pique your interest to look deeper into your own heart, it would be a good start, but introspection alone is not enough. In fact, alone, it is remarkably dangerous.

The pursuit of self-knowledge can easily become an idol of self-obsession. You can turn these instincts into forms of personality assessment and spend your days digging deeper into the fascinating world of your own uniqueness. That self-obsession usually leads you to one of two outcomes, both notoriously difficult to escape.

The more obvious is that you become like that tale of Narcissus, who fell in love with his own reflection in the pool. Captivated by what he saw, he wasted away staring at himself. You, too, can become obsessed with your own potential—lost in your own achievements and the possibility of your growth. You can craft programs and routines, buy self-help books, and watch endless motivational lectures to maximize every bit of your self-potential, a dizzying and heady pursuit of that promised self-actualization. Like Narcissus, you end up old, ugly, and still staring into that same pool.

But there is another risk, I think, more often realized. With every good intention, you become obsessed with constantly taking your spiritual temperature. You live in the perpetual insecurity of marking your own progress. You become an expert at your every fault. Soon, your spiritual life becomes that of Sisyphus, constantly rolling that boulder up the hill only to watch it roll back down and take up the same work again tomorrow. You get stuck in an endless loop of your own inabilities. Eventually, you'll probably give up and go back to ignore what you seem incapable of overcoming.

Self-knowledge isn't enough. It's prone to either inflate you with pride or deflate you with guilt. Neither changes you or offers a way beyond yourself. This is the problem with so much of the advice men receive. It traps them between the marketing pitch of their potential and the crushing weight of trying to make it happen by their own determination and discipline. Telling men to stand up straight and get their rooms in order may need to be said, but it becomes dangerous when motivated by personal potential and pride.

C. S. Lewis warned us about men who motivated maturity this way. He wrote, they "appeal to a boy's Pride, or, as they call it, his self-respect, to make him behave decently: many a man has overcome cowardice, or lust, or ill-temper, by learning to think that they are beneath his dignity—that is, by Pride." And as Lewis said, "It is Pride which has been the chief cause of misery in every nation and every family since the world began."[9]

The men who pull it off fall in love with themselves. The men who fail feel fated and cursed. Neither actually changes a man's soul. What we really need is something bigger than ourselves. We need enough self-knowledge to set us searching for something better than ourselves. We need more than expectations. We need, as so many gospel preachers have put it, not advice but news—good news. News of what has already been done for us.

WATCH THE TEACHING

Paul does not call Timothy to keep a close watch on his life alone. Timothy is to watch his life *and the teaching*. Paul is not describing some skill of teaching Timothy should continue to develop. Even in Greek, the article is emphatic—The Teaching. It was Paul's shorthand for the teaching which had been handed down by the apostles. It was the message of Jesus' death, resurrection, and return. Paul was urging Timothy to pay close attention to the gospel and to work out its meaning in the context of his self-watched life.

Paying attention to your life is offset by equal attention to what God has done and is doing. It is the great balancing of all things—my life set into the context of His salvation. As Flannery O'Connor put it, "To know oneself is, above all, to know what one lacks. It is to measure oneself against the Truth, and not the other way around."[10]

It is only by a growing knowledge and application of the gospel that we are capable of knowing ourselves. And it is also by knowing ourselves that we come to truly appreciate the remarkable power and grace of what Christ has done for us.

Ernest Gordon was not a follower of Christ when he arrived at that Japanese prison camp. He was when he left, and he went on to become a minister of the gospel he had received in those barbaric conditions. What changed Gordon was the power of the gospel, a story which pulled him out of his self-interest and opened the door to a world larger than even the conditions of that camp could take from him.

Stories began to break out across the prison camp. Men sacrificing for one another, risking their lives for others, and giving at their own expense. Gordon would later learn that one of his closest Christian friends was crucified by a Japanese officer irritated at the man's calm and unbreakable spirit. Those stories began to change men.

Gordon wrote,

It was dawning on us all—officers and other ranks alike—that the law of the jungle is not the law for man. We had seen for ourselves how quickly it could strip most of us of our humanity and reduce us to levels lower than the beasts . . . . Death was still with us—no doubt about that. But we were slowly being freed from its destructive grip. We were seeing for ourselves the sharp contrast between the forces that made for life and those that made for death. Selfishness, hatred, envy, jealousy, greed, self-indulgence, laziness and pride were all anti-life. Love, heroism, self-sacrifice, sympathy, mercy, integrity and creative faith, on the other hand, were the essence of life, turning mere existence into living in its truest sense. These were the gifts of God to men.[11]

It was the stories of sacrifice that cracked the door open to a possibility beyond themselves. The story changed them. It moved their hearts toward something better. So it is with the gospel story we have received. It changes us. As Paul said, "It is the power of God" (Rom. 1:16). And so, too, it invites us into a bigger and better world.

But just as you can lose your way with watching your life, so too, you can lose that sense of the gospel's power. You can lose the story.

Do you remember that conflict between Paul and Peter in the book of Acts? The apostle Peter had come to the city of Antioch where Paul was busy ministering to a growing Gentile church. Having previously seen a vision of unclean food descending from heaven and having heard the divine voice command him to take and eat, Peter had stepped out of the traditional Jewish boundaries and began to share meals with Gentile believers. Like

Peter, Paul was busy in Antioch eating and worshiping with these new Gentile converts. For devout Jews and many devout Jewish Christians, those actions violated proper Jewish distinctions and customs. Paul and Peter understood how the gospel was reshaping those boundaries.

Much to Paul's frustration, when prominent men from Jerusalem arrived, Peter began to draw back from his Gentile relationships. He would no longer join them in meals. Paul was furious. Remembering the event, he later wrote, "I opposed him to his face." Paul explained that Peter and those who followed his lead were "not in step with the truth of the gospel" (Gal. 2:11–14). Paul could have called their actions racist or prideful; he could have pointed out how they were acting against the Christian virtues of hospitality and generosity, but instead, Paul accused them of wandering away from the gospel path. Their practice was not in line with the gospel they believed.

Peter had lost the story. He had lost hold of what God was doing. Taking up a different story, he was embracing an entirely different set of values. Paul, like he had Timothy, urged Peter to look more closely at the gospel teaching.

It is always these two steps—left foot, right foot, self-knowledge, gospel-knowledge—that keep us moving in the right direction. Through honest reflection, we recognize a vulnerability or insufficiency in ourselves, and we turn to the gospel to find its correction. Likewise, the gospel will make some demand by the logic of its implications, and we search our hearts for compliance to it.

Sin may be a decision you make, but that lapse of judgment can always be traced deeper to a truth you believe more than you believe the gospel. Sin often seems like common sense—just the way the world works. It appears that way, even if just for a moment, because you assume you're on the right path. You lose your grip on the gospel story and start to believe an alternative one. Infused by this new story's logic and virtues, the story of the gospel seems strange and unrealistic. For those who fail to believe, it has long seemed foolish. The sign over Jesus' head read, "King of the Jews." The crowd thought it was a joke. Based on the story of the world they had believed, it was so absurd it couldn't be true. But it was. Lose the gospel story and all things turn inside out. As Chesterton is said to have put it, "It is because we are standing on our heads that Christ's philosophy seems upside down."[12]

Ultimately, it is this gospel story that serves as a corrective to each of the instincts I've outlined in this book, and I'm convinced you have little chance of righting your orientation to them without the gospel's power.

It is the gospel that gives you the security to embrace a self-suspicion necessary to overcome your immaturity and sarcasm. It is the gospel that offers you a better adventure through deeper commitments and discernment. It's the gospel that checks your ambition and teaches you to receive what you can't achieve by setting down your expectations and learning to rest. It's the gospel that exposes your pretending and teaches you the value of integrity over defending your reputation. And it is the gospel that keeps you engaged with this story of sacrifice and grace, rescuing you from your own apathy and pulling back into a life of faith.

Your instincts tell you a story. They offer an interpretation of where you are and where you should be headed. Remember Shakespeare's words: "All the world's a stage, And all the men and women merely players; They have their exits and their entrances; And one man in his time plays many parts."[13] Our instincts expect us to play their cast roles. But the gospel breaks their power by

THE 5 MASCULINE INSTINCTS

offering you another story by which to live. Shakespeare wrote of the world's stage, but the gospel transforms that stage into a better one, a heavenly one. You have a better part to play.

AN INFUSION OF CHARACTER

This is what it means to be a man, in the fullest potential of God's created intent. It's what it means to be maturing into Christlikeness. You must learn to know yourself. You must learn to know the gospel. Watch yourself and the teaching closely.

For the medieval church, Mary was often recognized as a person of perfect character and virtue. But even they acknowledged that ultimately character was an act of grace in which God moves upon the human heart. It is not achieved by determination or clever personal planning. It is infused into us as we turn toward God.

One medieval writer imagined Mary doing just that, turning in prayer toward God. The author wrote, "The greatness and nobility of this contemplation of God filled her full of reverent awe, and with this she saw herself so small and so humble, so simple and so poor in comparison with her Lord God that this reverent awe filled her with humility. And so, founded on this, she was filled with grace and with every kind of virtue."[14]

That is my prayer for you as well. As you turn to Christ and the gospel message of His sacrificial death and resurrection, you will catch an honest glimpse of yourself and of Him, and that vision will infuse virtue and character into you in a way never possible on your own. Those old instincts may hang around but, placed into the context of Christ's kingdom and the gospel's power, they lose something of their control over you. You are more a man for it.

Chapter 9

NOTHING LEFT TO PROVE

"Give a man a fish and you feed him for a day. Don't teach
a man to fish . . . and feed yourself. He's a grown man.
And fishing's not that hard."

RON SWANSON

"We have to grow into Scripture, like a young boy inheriting
his older brother's clothes and flopping around in them, but
he gradually builds out and grows up. Perhaps it's a measure
of our maturity when parts of Scripture that we found odd or
even repellent suddenly come up in a new light. Our sense is
overtaken by a sense of the whole thing, wide, multicolored,
and unspeakably powerful."

N.T. WRIGHT

Jesus once told the story of a landowner who came to pluck
figs from a tree in his vineyard. Inspecting the plant, he was
frustrated to discover that it still had not produced any fruit.
Having run out of patience, the man turned to his gardener and
complained. "Look, for three years now I have come seeking fruit
on this fig tree, and I find none. Cut it down. Why should it use
up the ground?" (Luke 13:7).

Fig trees are notoriously slow to produce fruit, some taking
as many as six years to start producing. Perhaps this owner had
been waiting three years beyond that expected coming of age,

possibly close to a decade of waiting and still no fruit. Pruning, watering, weeding, and waiting. By his evaluation, it was time to move on. Time to plant another tree. Time to find a better one. But the gardener responded, "Sir, let it alone this year also, until I dig around it and put on manure" (Luke 13:8).

That was the end of Jesus' story. A parable about spreading manure on a fruitless tree. We are never told what came of it. Did the manure work? Did the tree produce figs the following year? Did the owner cut it down anyway? That answer wasn't Jesus' point.

In a world ready to "cut it down," Jesus' parable speaks, "let it alone." Jesus saw the potential others missed. The servant in Jesus' parable was patient but not passive. He went to work, spreading more manure—waiting and working.

That isn't pleasant work. There's nothing exciting or charming about manure. No one gets a thrill from that chore. It stinks, but it also works. Manure produces life, life nurtured through what is waste. The process may be a slow, stinking mess, but from it will come the delicious taste of fresh figs. Maybe in just a little while longer. They wouldn't know until they waited some more. D. H. Lawrence wrote, "The fairest thing in nature, a flower, still has its roots in earth and manure."[1] And in waiting.

But we want it now. Lay hands on that barren tree, and let's pray in a miraculous budding of figs this year. Never mind all that talk of seasons, or age, or gestation. Instead, the servant dug around the tree, mixed in manure, and waited—believed.

I'm sure you have been frustrated by the limited fruit in your life. You are not who you imagine you could be. You probably won't wake up that better person tomorrow either. Maybe others have labeled you a similar waste of usable ground. Maybe

NOTHING LEFT TO PROVE

your whole life feels that way. It's going to take more than reading a book like this to change who you are. But, by God's grace, there is change, at times miraculous and spontaneous, but so much of the time painstakingly slow and nonobvious. Many men have lost hope along the way, having abandoned progress and accepted fruitlessness as the final verdict of

> It takes years for the tree to develop the roots capable of producing its fruit. The gardener cannot produce it; he must keep his attention on the soil.

their lives. They become frustrated by who they still are not and frustrated by a process that seems to have failed them.

Saint John of the Cross wisely noted,

> Some of these beginners, too, make little of their faults, and at other times become over-sad when they see themselves fall into them, thinking themselves to have been saints already; and thus they become angry and impatient with themselves. . . . Often they beseech God, with great yearnings, that He will take from them their imperfections and faults, but they do this that they may find themselves at peace, and may not be troubled by them, rather than for God's sake; not realizing that, if He should take their imperfections from them, they would probably become prouder and more presumptuous still.[2]

We may not like it, but waiting is so often the way Jesus works. Waiting is always the way fruit is grown. It takes years for the tree to develop the roots capable of producing its fruit. The gardener cannot produce it; he must keep his attention on the soil.

I've always loved that parable because Jesus identifies Himself with manure. It is the gospel, a compost of death to produce new life. The death of Christ is the fertilizer by which new life emerges—the Spirit working Christ into our hearts to bear new fruit. We spend our days raking more of that good news around the trunk of our lives and waiting to see what it produces.

Manhood is like that fruit. The by-product of growing in Christ is character and becoming the man God created you to be. It is cultivated character that allows the steward to keep at His work until that fruit is finally plucked. Like that fig tree, we can't do much more than enrich the soil and trust that it will work. Spend all your time obsessing over how to make yourself a man, and you will smother it with your pride or constantly taste the bitterness of your own failings. You will produce only the fruit of insecurity and be stunted in your future growth. You have your eyes on the wrong task. Get the shovel and get to work with the manure.

There is another way of saying this. You don't have anything to prove, at least not what you previously thought. Your job is not to convince yourself or anyone else that you are a man. Stop worrying so much about it. There is no test. There is no rite of passage. There is no badge to earn or trophy to secure it. The fruit will come with time; enjoy it as it does. But the work lies elsewhere.

You will soon discover the reward does too. For in your search for manhood, you may very well discover that it's not what you've really been searching for. That impulse to become a better man will lead you to something altogether better. The man you've been searching for is not yourself but Christ.

NOTHING TO PROVE

In his novel *Islands in the Stream*, Ernest Hemingway told the story of a father, Thomas Hudson, fishing with his three sons in the Gulf Stream just off the islands of the Bahamas. Trolling lines behind their 1930s diesel fishing boat, David, one of the sons, recognized the subtle movement of his line, evidence of a fish investigating the bait. Patiently, he waited for the fish to take it. Finally, feeling the tug of the fish's bite and with all of his adolescent weight, David set the hook. The line began to explode from his reel as the fish dove with the hook in its mouth. Thomas Hudson recognized by the speed at which the fish was pulling line from the reel that it was a large fish. His son was in for a fight.

The fight went on for hours. With the rod strapped to a harness around his waist, David sat fighting the fish for every inch. With all of his strength, he would lift the rod and scramble to take in line on the reel. He was sunburnt, sore, and bleeding from his feet as he braced them against the wood of the boat for leverage. Each time his father would ask if he wanted to continue, David nodded his head yes, unable to say anything more.

One of the other boys protested, "How much longer can you let him go on like this?" Thomas Hudson replied, "I would have stopped this long ago except that I know that if David catches this fish he'll have something inside him for all his life and it will make everything else easier."[3] The boy went on fighting. Fighting to catch a fish. Fighting to prove himself more than a boy.

Slowly the fish came up, and slowly the line came in. They pulled the fish alongside the boat and recognized that it was not just a large fish; it was the largest fish any of them had ever seen or, they knew immediately, ever would again. One of them slowly took the leader in his hand and began to lift up on the fish so another could gaffe it in the side. The line gave some and then gave again. They watched as the hook tore through the fish's jaw and came loose, blowing now in the wind. The fish lay suspended beside the boat for a moment and then slid down into the depth below them. The fish was gone. Lost.

Exhausted, frustrated, and overwhelmed, David cried. So did the other boys. As the boat made its way home, they opened bottles of Coca-Cola and began to talk. One said, "If you'd have caught him you'd have been probably the most famous young boy in the world."

David spoke, "I'll tell you sometime how it was."

"Tell now," they urged him.

"I'm tired now and besides it sounds crazy."

"Tell now, tell a little bit," they pleaded.

"Well," David said, his eyes shut tight, "in the worst parts, when I was the tiredest I couldn't tell which was him and which was me. . . . Then I began to love him more than anything on earth."

David explained he didn't care that he had lost the fish. "I don't care about records. I just thought I did." He admitted. "I'm glad that he's all right and that I'm all right. We aren't enemies."[4]

He had discovered something more than his first instinct, something better. It wasn't landing a fish that marked his passing from childhood into manhood; it was the realization he had it and didn't need a fish to prove it. It isn't about records or achievements. It's not about recognition or status. It's not about skill or physique. It's not ever something you prove, but something you possess—something you discover. Something there without the need to prove it.

As Peter put it, "His divine power has granted to us all things that pertain to life and godliness, through the knowledge of him who called us to his own glory and excellence" (2 Peter 1:3).

You have nothing to prove.

When I stop and think about it, all of the men I respect most don't seem to care that much about proving it either. They don't seem all that interested in making sure others recognize it in them. There is something quieter in them. Something more secure. Something they possess which can't ever really be proven anyway.

You need not land the fish to know you can. You don't need the proof to have lived the tale. And maybe most importantly, the pursuit is best when it gives way to something far more meaningful than you originally sought. That thing you so desperately needed turns out only to be the path by which you discovered something far better.

What you have is something better. A better goal. A better path. A better strength. A better instinct. A better manhood.

Eugene Peterson explains it as wisely and plainspoken as anyone I know. He wrote, "One way to define spiritual life is getting so tired and fed up with yourself you go on to something better, which is following Jesus."[5]

Keep watching your life. Keep watching your doctrine. Keep spreading that manure.

ACKNOWLEDGMENTS

I owe the biggest thanks to my wife for her faithful support in watching me stumble my way through so many of these lessons and attempting to write them down for others. She knows above all others how much work has gone into this pursuit and how much I owe her for helping me stay the course. To write well one must first live well; you help me do that every day. Thank you for helping me become a better man and sticking with me when I've failed to live up to my own advice.

To Pastor Alan Baker I owe the thanks of wise and faithful counsel. Our biweekly calls have not only helped me complete this work but grow in my own integrity and self-honesty. To Justus Boever who has always been my first reader and one of the most insightful friends a writer could hope to have. To Mick Silva who encouraged me to write when I had little more than a few pages of paragraphs and a crazy idea that I could do it. Thanks for persevering so long with me. To Janet Grant who has offered steadfast and wise counsel at every step of this endeavor. I'd still be lost in those Mt. Hermon woods without your guidance and resolve.

And to the men and women of Bent Oak Church. I am and will always be your pastor first. Your weekly encouragements, worship, and prayers have sustained me through sickness and celebration. So much of what I know about following Christ has been discovered with you. I am deeply grateful to God for bringing us all together.

NOTES

CHAPTER 1: MEN, MEAT, AND THE MASCULINE MALAISE

1. Attila Pohlmann, "Threatened at the Table: Meat Consumption, Maleness and Men's Gender Identities," University of Hawaii at Manoa, May 2014.

2. Ibid., 21.

3. Ibid., 28.

4. "2015–2020 Dietary Guidelines for Americans, 8th Edition," US Department of Health and Human Services and US Department of Agriculture, last updated December 29, 2020, https://health.gov/our-work/food-nutrition/previous-dietary-guidelines/2015.

5. Angus Chen, "Origins of Male Domination May Lie in Food," *Scientific American*, May 1, 2017, http://scientificamerican.com/article/origins-of-male-domination-may-lie-in-food.

6. Victoria Gagliardo-Silver, "Fragile Masculinity Says Meat Is Manly. If We Don't Challenge That, People Will Die, and the Earth Will Be Irreversibly Damaged," *The Independent*, April 4, 2019, independent .co.uk/voices/fragile-masculinity-mean-eaters-death-vegan-vegetarian-earth-a8855331.html.

7. Stephanie Pappas, "APA Issues First-Ever Guidelines for Practice with Men and Boys," *Monitor on Psychology*, American Psychological Association, January 2019, 34, https://www.apa.org/monitor/2019/01/ce-corner.

8. Michael Ian Black, "The Boys Are Not All Right," *New York Times*, February 21, 2018, nytimes.com/2018/02/21/opinion/boys-violence-shootings-guns.html.

9. Walker Percy, *The Moviegoer* (New York: Open Road Media, 2011), 228.

10. C. S. Lewis, *The Abolition of Man* (New York: HarperOne, 1974), 34.

11. C. S. Lewis, *Christian Reflections* (Grand Rapids: Eerdmans Publishing Company, 2014), 60.
12. Lewis, *The Abolition of Man*, 34ff.
13. Friedrich Nietzsche, *The Case of Wagner: The Twilight of the Idols; Nietzsche Contra Wagner*, trans. Thomas Common (New York: Macmillan Publishers, 1908), 43.

CHAPTER 2: LEARNING TO RECOGNIZE YOUR INSTINCTS

1. William Shakespeare, "As You Like It," Folger Shakespeare Library. https://shakespeare.folger.edu/shakespeares-works/as-you-like-it/.
2. Paul A. Taylor, "Sympathy and Insight in Aristotle's Poetics," *The Journal of Aesthetics and Art Criticism* 66, No. 3 (Summer 2008): 268.
3. Eugene H. Peterson, *Eat This Book: a Conversation in the Art of Spiritual Reading* (Colorado Springs: Eerdmans, 2006), 41.
4. Erich Auerbach, *Mimesis: The Representation of Reality in Western Literature* (Princeton, NJ: Princeton University Press, 2003), 15.
5. C. S. Lewis, *Mere Christianity* (New York: HarperOne, 1996), 71.
6. Ibid.
7. Ibid.
8. Ibid., 72.
9. N. T. Wright, *After You Believe: Why Christian Character Matters* (New York: HarperOne, 2010), 30.
10. Lewis, *Mere Christianity*, 11.

CHAPTER 3: SARCASM: THE HUMOR OF OUR AGE

1. John Haiman, *Talk Is Cheap: Sarcasm, Alienation, and the Evolution of Language* (New York: Oxford University Press, 1998).
2. John Knowles, *A Separate Peace* (New York: Scribner, 1987), 29.
3. Flannery O'Connor, *Wise Blood: A Novel* (New York: Farrar, Straus and Giroux, 1990), 229.
4. Oswald Chambers, *My Utmost for His Highest* (Uhrichsville, OH: Barbour Publishing, 1963), December 7.
5. Ibid.
6. Robert Alter, *The Five Books of Moses, Translated with Notes and Commentary* (New York: W. W. Norton & Company, 1996), 29.

7. James Montgomery Boice, *Genesis: An Expositional Commentary*, vol. 1 (Grand Rapids: Baker Books, 1998), 258.

8. C. S. Lewis, *The Abolition of Man* (New York: HarperOne, 1971), 16.

9. Ibid., 11.

10. Ibid., 26.

11. Thomas Merton, *The Seven Storey Mountain: An Autobiography of Faith* (Orlando: Harcourt, 1998), 3.

12. The Society of Gilbert Keith Chesterton. "What's Wrong with the World?," The Apostolate of Common Sense, April 29, 2012, https://www.chesterton.org/wrong-with-world/.

13. "Eugene Peterson: Translating the Beatitudes," YouTube, Navpress, December 19, 2017, youtube.com/watch?v=b80KhqMeM2A.

14. Plato and Xenophon, *Apologies*, trans. Mark Kremer (Indianapolis, IN: Hackett Publishing Company, 2012), 6. While widely quoted, this quotation is really a paraphrase of Socrates's words, "I am wiser than this man; it is likely that neither of us knows anything worthwhile, but he thinks he knows something when he does not, whereas when I do not know, neither do I think I know; so I am likely to be wiser than he to this small extent, that I do not think I know when I do not know."

15. *Letters (83–130)*, ed. Roy Joseph Deferrari, trans. Wilfrid Parsons, vol. 18, The Fathers of the Church (Washington, DC: The Catholic University of America Press, 1953), 282.

16. Kendra Cherry, "The Dunning-Kruger Effect," Verywell Mind, June 14, 2019, https://www.verywellmind.com/an-overview-of-the-dunning-kruger-effect-4160740.

17. Ibid.

18. David Dunning, "We Are All Confident Idiots," *Pacific Standard*, October 27, 2014, updated June 14, 2017, https://psmag.com/social-justice/confident-idiots-92793.

19. *Letters (83–130)*, 282.

20. John Calvin, *Institutes of the Christian Religion*, trans. Henry Beveridge (Peabody, MA: Hendrickson Publishers, 2008), 5.

21. Derek Rishmawy, "Meekness Is Not Weakness," *Christianity Today*, May 17, 2019, christianitytoday.com/ct/2019/june/meekness-is-not-weakness.html.

22. David Molyneaux, "'Blessed Are the Meek, for They Shall Inherit the Earth': An Aspiration Applicable to Business?," *Journal of Business Ethics* 48, no. 4 (December 2003): 347.

23. Xenophon, *On Horsemanship* (Plano, TX: SMK, 2018), 19.

24. Charles Spurgeon, *Morning and Evening* (Peabody, MA: Hendrickson, 1991), 45.

25. Elisabeth Elliot, *The Journals of Jim Elliot* (Grand Rapids: Fleming H. Revell, 1978), 174.

CHAPTER 4: ADVENTURE: CULTIVATING NEW EYES

1. Skift Research, "Global Report on Adventure Tourism," World Tourism Organization, November 2014, https://skift.com/wp-content/uploads/2014/11/unwto-global-report-on-adventure-tourism.pdf.

2. Joseph Campbell with Bill Moyers, *The Power of Myth* (New York: Anchor, 1991), 152.

3. Ibid., 115, 150.

4. Francis Spufford, *Unapologetic: Why, Despite Everything, Christianity Can Still Make Surprising Emotional Sense* (New York: HarperOne, 2012), 28.

5. Michael Frank, "Yeats, a Poet Who Kept Trying On Different Identities," *New York Times*, August 6, 1999, https://www.nytimes.com/1999/08/06/books/yeats-a-poet-who-kept-trying-on-different-identities.html.

6. Timothy Jones, *Awake My Soul: Practical Spirituality for Busy People* (New York: Random House, 1984), 64.

7. Rainer Maria Rilke, *Letters to a Young Poet* (London: W. W. Norton, 1962), 17.

8. J. R. R. Tolkien, *The Lord of the Rings* (New York: Houghton Mifflin, 2004), 711.

9. Ibid.

10. G. K. Chesterton, *Tremendous Trifles* (Mineola, NY: Dover, 2007), 96.

11. David Jackman, *Judges, Ruth* (Dallas: Word, 1991), 243.

CHAPTER 5: AMBITION: A PROMISED LAND LOST

1. Martin Luther King Jr., "I Have a Dream" (address delivered at the March on Washington for Jobs and Freedom), The Martin Luther King, Jr. Research and Education Institute, https://kinginstitute.stanford.edu/

king-papers/documents/i-have-dream-address-delivered-march-washington-jobs-and-freedom.

2. Martin Luther King Jr., "I've Been to the Mountaintop," The Martin Luther King, Jr. Research and Education Institute, April 3, 1968, https://kinginstitute.stanford.edu/encyclopedia/ive-been-mountaintop.

3. Aaron Wildavsky, *The Nursing Father: Moses as Political Leader* (Tuscaloosa, AL: The University of Alabama Press, 1984), 153.

4. Midrash Rabbah, Exodus 1:26.

5. William Shakespeare, "Song: 'Under the Greenwood Tree," Poetry Foundation, https://www.poetryfoundation.org/poems/47423/song-under-the-greenwood-tree.

6. John Calvin, *John Calvin's Bible Commentaries on the Psalms 119–150* (Altenmunster, Loschberg: Jazzybee Verlag Jurgen Beck, 2017), 95.

7. Victor Hugo, *Les Miserables* (New York: Sterling, 2003), 63.

8. Søren Kierkegaard, *Provocations: Spiritual Writings of Kierkegaard* (Walden, NY: Plough, 2002), 5.

9. "Dietrich Bonhoeffer: German Theologian and Resister," *Christianity Today*, https://www.christianitytoday.com/history/people/martyrs/dietrich-bonhoeffer.html.

10. Dietrich Bonhoeffer, *Life Together: The Classic Exploration of Faith in Community* (New York: Harper & Row, 1954), 27.

11. Ibid., 28.

12. Alexander Pope, "Elegy to the Memory of an Unfortunate Lady," Poetry Foundation, https://www.poetryfoundation.org/poems/44891/elegy-to-the-memory-of-an-unfortunate-lady.

13. William Shakespeare, *Henry VIII*, Act III, Scene 2, Open Source Shakespeare, https://www.opensourceshakespeare.org/views/plays/play_view.php?WorkID=henry8&Act=3&Scene=2&Scope=scene.

14. Eugene Peterson, *A Long Obedience in the Same Direction* (Downers Grove, IL: IVP, 2000), 151.

15. Ibid., 153.

16. Avivah Gottlieb Zornberg, *Moses: A Human Life* (New Haven, CT: Yale University Press, 2016), 192.

17. Leo Tolstoy, *Essays, Letters and Miscellanies* (Rockville, MD: Wildside, 2021), 157.

18. C. S. Lewis, *Letters to an American Lady* (Grand Rapids: Eerdmans, 1967), 50.

19. *Chariots of Fire*, directed by Hugh Hudson (The Ladd Company/Warner Bros., 1981).

20. Ibid.

21. Sally Magnusson, *The Flying Scotsman: The Eric Liddell Story* (Cheltenham, UK: The History Press, 2007), 160.

22. Bonhoeffer, *Life Together*, 99.

CHAPTER 6: REPUTATION: THE IMAGE OF A KING

1. Augustus C. Buell, *History of Andrew Jackson: Pioneer, Patriot, Soldier, Politician, President* (New York: Charles Scribner's Sons, 1904), 204.

2. Cumberland Valley Tree Service, "When to Preserve and When to Plant Anew: The White House's Jackson Magnolia and Gettysburg's Witness Trees," CVTS-L, cvtslandscape.com/white-house-jackson-magnolia.

3. Parker J. Palmer, *A Hidden Wholeness: The Journey Toward an Undivided Life* (San Francisco: Jossey-Bass, 2004), 44.

4. Steven E. Landsburg, "Short Changed: Why Do Tall People Make More Money?," *Slate*, March 25, 2002, slate.com/culture/2002/03/it-pays-to-be-tall.html.

5. Lea Winerman, "'Thin Slices' of Life," *Monitor on Psychology*, American Psychological Association, March 2005, https://www.apa.org/monitor/mar05/slices.

6. Chad Boutin, "To Determine Election Outcomes, Study Says Snap Judgments Are Sufficient," Princeton University, October 22, 2007, https://www.princeton.edu/news/2007/10/22/determine-election-outcomes-study-says-snap-judgments-are-sufficient.

7. Hialmer Day Gould and Edward Louis Hessenmueller, *Best Thoughts of Best Thinkers* (Ann Arbor, MI: University of Michigan Library, 1904), 429.

8. Heloise Hawthorne, *Contemplations from the Writings of Elbert Hubbard* (Whitefish, MT: Kessinger, 2010), 4.

9. "Quotations from Mark Twain [1835-1910]," Working Minds, https://working-minds.com/MTquotes.htm.

10. Walter Brueggemann, *Interpretation: First and Second Samuel* (Louisville, KY: Westminster John Knox, 1990), 145.

11. Dietrich Bonhoeffer, *Life Together: The Classic Exploration of Faith in Community* (New York: Harper & Row, 1954), 110.

12. Søren Kierkegaard, *Either/Or: A Fragment of Life* (New York: Penguin, 1992), 447.

13. "Integrity," Webster's 1913 Dictionary, http://www.websters1913.com/words/Integrity.

14. Leo Tolstoy, *The Death of Ivan Ilyich* (New York: New American Library, 2003), 113.

15. Ibid., 121.

16. Ibid., 144.

17. Baruch Halpern, *David's Secret Demons: Messiah, Murderer, Traitor, King* (Grand Rapids: Eerdmans, 2001), 6.

18. Thomas Merton, *No Man Is an Island* (Boston: Mariner, 2002), 140.

19. G. K. Chesterton, *The Man Who Was Orthodox* (London: D. Dobson, 1963), 158.

20. Saint Augustine, *The Confessions* (New York: New City Press, 2001), 181.

CHAPTER SEVEN: APATHY: A WORLD TOO WIDE

1. Stephen Hawking, *A Brief History of Time* (New York: Bantam, 2017), 149.

2. James Gleick, *The Information: A History, A Theory, A Flood* (New York: Vintage, 2011), 282.

3. *The Count of Monte Cristo*, directed by Kevin Reynolds (2002; Reliance Pictures).

4. William Shakespeare, *As You Like It*, Folger Shakespeare Library, https://shakespeare.folger.edu/shakespeares-works/as-you-like-it/.

5. Elaine Cumming and William Earl Henry, *Growing Old: Aging and Old Age* (North Stratford, NH: Ayer, 1979).

6. Mark Twain, *Mark Twain at Your Fingertips: A Book of Quotations* (Mineola, NY: Dover, 2009), 228.

7. Reinhold Niebuhr, *Discerning the Signs of the Times: Sermons for Today and Tomorrow* (New York: Charles Scribner's Sons, 1946), 111.

8. Gil Greengross, "Humor and Aging—A Mini-Review," *Gerontology* 59, no. 5 (2013): 448–53.

9. C. S. Lewis, *The Screwtape Letters* (New York: HarperCollins, 2001), 61.

10. Neil Postman, *Amusing Ourselves to Death: Public Discourse in the Age of Show Business* (New York: Penguin, 2005), xix.

11. "Harmful Masculinity and Violence," *In the Public Interest*, American Psychological Association, September 2018, https://www.apa.org/pi/about/newsletter/2018/09/harmful-masculinity.

12. Agatha Christie, *The Under Dog and Other Stories* (New York: Harper-Collins, 2012), 51.

13. Ron Dicker, "Mark Hamill Rips His Role in 'Last Jedi': 'He's Not My Luke Skywalker,'" *HuffPost*, December 22, 2017, https://www.huffpost.com/entry/mark-hamill-last-jedi-luke-skywalker_n_5a3cf644e4b025f99e16864d.

14. Ibid.

15. John Gray, *The Silence of Animals: On Progress and Other Modern Myths* (New York: Farrar, Straus and Giroux, 2013), 75.

16. Ibid.

17. "Rashi on Genesis 22:2," Sefaria, sefaria.org/Rashi_on_Genesis.22.2.4?lang=bi&with=Midrash&lang2=en.

18. Eugene H. Peterson, *The Jesus Way: A Conversation on the Ways That Jesus Is the Way* (Grand Rapids: Eerdmans, 2007), 56–57.

19. Ibid., 49.

20. C. S. Lewis, *The Four Loves* (New York: HarperCollins, 1960), 155.

21. C. G. Jung, *Psychology and Religion: West and East* (New York: Bollingen Foundation, 1958), 257–58.

22. Richard Dawkins, *The God Delusion* (Boston: Mariner, 2008), 274–75.

23. Hannah Arendt, *The Life of the Mind: The Groundbreaking Investigation on How We Think* (New York: Harcourt, 1978), 180.

24. Peterson, *The Jesus Way*, 45.

CHAPTER EIGHT: THE REAL WORK AHEAD

1. Ernest Gordon, *To End All Wars: A True Story about the Will to Survive and the Courage to Forgive* (Grand Rapids: Zondervan, 2002), 73.

2. Ibid.

3. Ibid.

4. Ibid., 114.

5. Ibid.

6. Ibid., 101.

7. George MacDonald, *Phantastes: A Faerie Romance* (Grand Rapids: Eerdmans, 2000), 166.

8. John Owen, *The Works of John Owen,* vol. VI (London: Johnstone and Hunter, 1851), 162.

9. C. S. Lewis, *Mere Christianity* (New York: Simon & Schuster, 1996), 111.

10. Flannery O'Connor, *O'Connor: Collected Works* (New York: Library of America, 1988), 806.

11. Gordon, *To End All Wars,* 105.

12. G. K. Chesterton, quoted in Peter Kreeft, "Part Two: Happiness: The First Three Beatitudes," *Catholic Education Resource Center*, http://www.catholiceducation.org/en/religion-and-philosophy/philosophy/part-two-happiness-the-first-three-beatitudes.html.

13. William Shakespeare, *As You Like It*, Folger Shakespeare Library, https://shakespeare.folger.edu/shakespeares-works/as-you-like-it/.

14. Julian of Norwich, *Revelations of Divine Love* (Oxford: Oxford University Press, 2015), 48.

CHAPTER NINE: NOTHING LEFT TO PROVE

1. D. H. Lawrence, *The Complete Poems of D. H. Lawrence* (Hertfordshire, UK: Wordsworth, 1994), 625.

2. St. John of the Cross, *Dark Night of the Soul* (Mineola, NY: Dover, 2003), 7.

3. Ernest Hemingway, *Islands in the Stream* (New York: Simon & Schuster, 1970), 132.

4. Ibid., 143.

5. Mark Galli, "Spirituality for All the Wrong Reasons: Eugene Peterson Talks about Lies and Illusions That Destroy the Church," *Christianity Today*, March 4, 2005, https://www.christianitytoday.com/ct/2005/march/spirituality-for-all-the-wrong-reasons.html.

THE LOVE SHE CRAVES,
THE CONFIDENCE YOU NEED

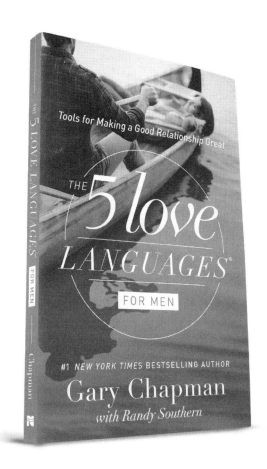

The 5 Love Languages® has sold over 10 million copies because it is simple, practical, and effective. In this men's edition packed with helpful illustrations and creative pointers, Gary Chapman speaks straight to the needs, challenges, and interests of husbands who want to master the art of loving their wives.

978-0-8024-1272-0 | also available as an eBook

SPIRITUAL DISCIPLINES ARE TO THE BELIEVER WHAT MEDICAL SCHOOL IS TO THE DOCTOR.

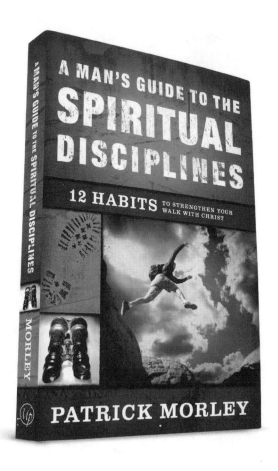

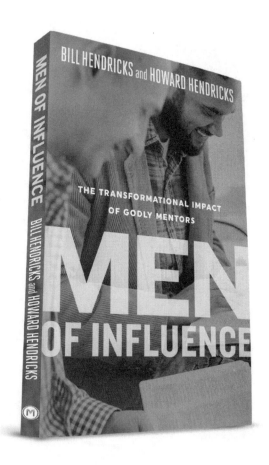